Dedication

To Christopher, Zachary and Mackenzie…

For the gift of time travel. And letting me share the journey with them.

And to my parents, Mr. and Mrs. D.K. Marsh, for placing into my outstretched hands a ball and glove, on a warm spring day in 1958.

Foreword

Don Marsh's "101 Things You Can Teach Your Kids About Baseball" has become a classic in the world of youth baseball, explaining the most basic elements of playing this game in language both child and adult can understand.

Coach Don's years of experience as player, parent, and coach gives him insight into the nuances of teaching baseball to kids that most professional coaches are lacking. A must-read for every beginning baseball parent!

Dave Destler, Publisher
Junior Baseball magazine

For more information on Junior Baseball magazine,
call Toll-Free 1-888 IT'S A HIT (1-888-487-2448).

Or visit their Web site @ **www.juniorbaseball.com.**

Table of Contents

Introduction -

Chances are, baseball was something you shared with your Dad - playing catch in the backyard or watching "The Game of the Week" on TV. Now you have kids of your own, whose curiosity and enthusiasm for the game remind you of that warm spring day in 1973... or 1967... or 1959, when you were young and baseball became your first love.

If that sounds at all familiar, then **101 Things You Can Teach Your Kids About Baseball** is the book written just for you.

My name is Don Marsh. I've spent more than 25 years playing, teaching or coaching baseball. Playing the game was great fun. Teaching my own kids is even better.

That's why I wrote **101 Things...** To share that love of baseball - and family time well spent - with other parents who know the fun that can be found in a simple game of pitch and catch, sprinkled with generous amounts of green grass, blue sky and sunshine.

After all these years I've decided that in the end, what playing baseball with your kids really is all about - is **time traveling.** Allowing yourself to be transported all the way back to Saturday afternoons when the world was no bigger than your neighborhood ballpark. But this time, you get to take the journey with your kids along for the ride.

This book is written for all the Dads & Moms who take the time and share the responsibility of passing the game of baseball on to the generation that has followed. To your kids. To anybody's kids. Doesn't matter. The reward is in the act itself.

With my thanks....

And unyielding admiration,

Don Marsh

P.S. Oh, and about that title... I've counted them up, and there really aren't "101 Things You Can Teach Your Kids About Baseball" in this book. There's at least <u>747 of them.</u>

The "Baseball Tips" System_{tm}

Whether your involvement these days is the time spent - no, make that **invested** - playing with your kids each week, or you're one of the brave souls who accept the challenge and reward of coaching an entire team, **101 Things You Can Teach Your Kids About Baseball** is guaranteed to help your family enjoy the game that has brought parents & kids together for generations.

101 Things... is written in simple, understandable language that makes teaching easy and learning fun. No need to sort through pages and pages of long text to find what you're looking for, the unique "Baseball Tips" System_{tm} allows you to use **either age or experience** in selecting the tips that will be most helpful to your kids. Quickly. Easily. Every time.

You'll find the complete System_{tm} listed at the beginning of each chapter. You'll also find that **Drills** are called out separately, as are special items called **"FastFacts",** which are designed to show the similarities between the way baseball is played at the professional and youth baseball levels. (Quick question: If home plate is 17 inches wide in the major leagues, how wide is it for your kids? Answer: 17 inches. Moral: the game is the same.) There's also a series of **illustrations** that will help you and your kids understand key points. The instructional portion of the book concludes with **four chapters written just for the volunteer coach.**

The book ends with a special **"letter" to the parents,** describing the value of baseball as a family activity, followed by some **Diary pages** that will help you record all the moments you'll share with your kids for all the baseball seasons to come.

Have fun.

And remember, it's only a game...

In the summer of 1965, I was a lefthanded pitcher for some Babe Ruth All-Stars that had defeated teams from throughout the western United States on our way to the championship game, played on a hot August evening in Stockton, California.

I pitched 10 innings, gave up two hits and struck out 18, leaving the game in a scoreless tie. In the 11th, on a couple of walks, an error and a swinging bunt, we lost, 1 to 0.

Several weeks later, on a smoggy Tuesday in Los Angeles, we were guests of the Dodgers for a late-season game against the Cubs. Sandy Koufax started for the Dodgers, opposed by journeyman lefthander Bob Hendley.

I watched Hendley pitch the game of his career, giving up only one hit on a broken-bat, wrong-field single by Lou Johnson. He lost, 1 to 0.

It was the night Koufax threw his perfect game.

That's baseball...

Chapter 1

Pitching

In the language of baseball there are "throwers" and there are "pitchers". Throwers have strong arms. Pitchers have been taught how to put those strong arms to best use. Here lies what probably will be the most difficult, frustrating, and in the end, rewarding part of teaching your kids how to play the game: Crossing that elusive threshold wherein a thrower is magically transformed into a pitcher. Relax, it's not as hard as it sounds. Not when you begin the journey this way...

The "Baseball Tips" Systemᴛᴍ:

	Age 10 & Under/Beginner
	Age 12 & Under/Intermediate
	Age 16 & Under/Advanced
DRILLS	Are called out

TIP LEVEL	PITCHING
	Start with both feet on the mound and enough cleat hanging over the front edge so the pivot foot can easily rotate 90 degrees to a spot inside the mound.
	Don't pitch from on top of the mound. The leverage gained from pushing off the inside means extra MPH on the fastball.
	With the weight on the pivot foot, the motion begins by simply stepping back. Not a big step, just enough to briefly transfer the weight from one foot to the other

(continued)

TIP LEVEL	PITCHING

 before the body rocks forward again. There are four parts to the pitching motion. This is the first - and least important - of the four.

 Some kids like stepping sideways, or parallel to the mound. This makes it more difficult to align the body with home plate. It's OK for these kids to use a 45-degree step, neither sideways nor straight back, until they feel comfortable stepping straight back.

 As the pivot foot moves inside the mound and the hips turn, the front knee swings all the way around until it's even with the back knee. Picture a flamingo wearing a baseball glove. This is called the **Balance Point** and it's the second - and most important - part of the motion because it puts the weight directly over the back leg before driving toward home plate. When young pitchers can't throw strikes, not reaching their Balance Point is often the reason why.

DRILL Once they get to the Balance Point, have your kids pause for a few seconds before continuing the motion. This is something they will be able to do only if the Balance Point has been fully reached. If they ask why the back leg is so important to a pitcher, have them compare the muscle in their arm to the one in their thigh. Now have them tell you which muscle is bigger. End of conversation.

 Of all the body parts involved in the pitching motion, the hands might be the least important. It's probably best to let your kids decide how high they want to "pump" with them, especially if they're just starting out.

| TIP LEVEL | PITCHING |

Remember, though, the **best pitching motion** is the simplest one, a motion that's economical in both movement and energy. Have them find a comfort zone with their hands, whether it's waist-high, chest-high, or over the head, and just go on from there.

Hands may not be all that important, but shoulders are. They should be level on the drive toward home plate. Teach your kids to keep the **front shoulder closed,** letting it point the way to the catcher's glove. Pitchers who open up with the front shoulder too soon are destined for two things: An inability to throw strikes consistently and getting to know the neighborhood orthopedics guy on a first-name basis.

FastFact: 40% of all injuries are to a pitcher's shoulder, more than to elbow, hand or any other part of the body. Yes, the human body **was** designed to throw a ball, but **underhand,** not overhand.

It's important kids also learn to keep the **front elbow up** during the delivery. Dropping the elbow results in a higher release point, which means the ball will stay up in the strike zone. Or out of it. For the advanced kids, dropping the front elbow also takes away the leverage needed to get the proper rotation on the curve ball. More on that later.

We've now made our way into the third part of the pitching motion: **the Release.** Don't be surprised if this winds up being the most confusing for your kids, since more things are happening here than during any other part of the delivery. Some things to look for: The back **hip rotating** forward, releasing the power generated by the back leg. The **front foot pointing** toward home plate when it lands. The **throwing hand directly** over

(continued)

TIP LEVEL	PITCHING

the front foot at the point of release. The **elbow** at least **shoulder-high.** The **shoulders parallel** to the mound, leaving the upper body facing home plate.

Use the analogy of hands on a clock to teach your kids the proper release point. Tell them to imagine there's an imaginary clock surrounding home plate. For right handers, it's **somewhere around 1 o'clock.** For left handers, **somewhere around 11 o'clock.** Anything lower, or more side-arm, than that will likely result in loss of control on fastballs, less break on curve balls and, worst of all, arm problems somewhere down the road.

There's an imaginary line running from the pivot foot to the catcher's glove. For a right-hander, the landing point with the front foot should be on or just to the left of that imaginary line. For a left-hander, on or just to the right of it. Landing past that line means the pitcher has opened up the front shoulder too soon. Landing before it means he's throwing against his body. Good pitchers use the same delivery every time, and a key to that is having the same landing point.

An inability to throw strikes also can be the product of a stride that's either too short or too long. A **short stride** means the ball is released too far back and will stay up in the strike zone. A **long stride** means the ball is released too far forward and will stay down.

FastFact: Major league pitchers look for a stride that's as much as 90% of their height (72 inches tall = 65-inch stride). With most kids, an 80% stride (60 inches tall = 48-inch stride) is a good target to shoot for. Understand this is not an absolute, given as how kids have a remarkable tendency to come in all shapes and sizes, and as a result, for shorter kids especially, even a 50% stride might be good enough for now.

TIP LEVEL	PITCHING

DRILL

Draw a big "X" to mark the landing point the first time your kids throw a strike. See how often they land in the same spot each time thereafter. Pitching is about two things: **Mechanics & Attitude.** This is a terrific way to help with the Mechanics.

All of which brings us to the last of the four parts of the pitching motion: the **Follow-Through.** The most important thing you can teach your kids is to make sure the throwing hand comes all the way down, brushing against the opposite knee. Right-hand-to-left-knee, or left-hand-to-right-knee. Lots of kids end the motion with the throwing hand down at their side, in effect short-arming the ball, which in turn robs them of both accuracy and velocity. A sure sign of a thrower who's not yet learned to be a pitcher.

Another way to teach your kids the proper follow-through is to use the clock analogy once again. If the proper release point for right handers is around 1 o'clock, then the follow-through should be around 7 o'clock. For left handers, whose release point is around 11 o'clock, the follow-through is around 5 o'clock.

Also look to see that the trailing leg has come all the way around, landing at a spot even with the front leg.

At the end of the Follow-Through your pitcher should be squared-up, facing home plate, and ready to catch the ball. In other words, he should look just like a fielder. Which is what he's just become.

(continued)

TIP LEVEL	PITCHING

DRILL

Here's a great two-player drill. Have one kneel in front of the other, just in front of where the pitcher would be at the end of a complete motion. The one kneeling tells the other to "...Give me five" (see illustration) on the Follow-Through, placing his hand by the pitcher's opposite knee. This simple drill is great for a couple of reasons: **(1)** Helps kids remember to complete the Follow-Through, and, **(2)** Teaches an extra wrist-snap that translates into more velocity on the fastball. This also can be done by having the pitcher use a short piece of towel, holding it by the fingertips.

Teach your kids not to rush the motion - to just let everything work in a slow, easy rhythm, with each of the four parts unfolding at the **same pace.** Sometimes it helps to stand alongside, clapping out a steady beat, as if you were the metronome and they were practicing at the piano. This is especially helpful for kids who are having a hard time throwing strikes, since rushing one part of the motion guarantees problems in the other three.

When you add it all up, pitching is a lot like the real estate business, where success measured by three things: Location, location and location. Make sure your kids understand that **velocity comes in a very poor third place, behind accuracy and movement on the ball,** when evaluating pitching ability. Teach them to throw strikes as a first order of business and everything after that will be a whole lot easier. For you and for them.

NOW LET'S TALK ABOUT DIFFERENT PITCHES:

First, a quick editorial: Experience suggests that young pitchers often fall in love with curve balls. Sore arms are not the only problems that can develop. It's also hard for kids to develop the arm strength they'll need down the road when all they want to do is throw off-speed pitches now. Sixty miles an hour is a pretty good fastball in Little League, but it's doesn't buy much at the high school level. Moral of the story: The potential damage from throwing too many curve balls isn't only to a kid's arm, it's to his head, as well. Here are **five words** that should be etched in the mind of every young pitcher: **Make Them Hit the Fastball.**

The basic fastball grip is called the **Four-Seam.** The same grip, by the way, that should be taught to infielders, outfielders, anyone in the business of throwing a baseball. It's called the Four-Seam grip because it allows four fingers (thumb, 1st 2nd and 3rd) to be in contact with the ball **across** **the seams,** where the seams are at their widest point. Many kids know this is the proper way to grip a baseball. Not many know the reason why: This grip makes the ball **spin backward** once it leaves the hand, allowing it to travel farther and straighter. For pitchers who are blessed with both strong arms and good mechanics, this grip will also make the ball **rise.**

The other way to grip a fastball is **with the seams,** along their narrowest point. This is the **Two-Seam, or sinking fastball,** grip. The thumb is placed underneath the ball. In time, your kids will learn to use the thumb as a rudder, moving it left or right, to make the ball move to either side. The sinking fastball is perfect for pitchers not gifted with real strong arms. What you get with the sinker is lots and lots of ground balls. Not a bad weapon for a pitcher to have in his arsenal.

(continued)

TIP LEVEL	PITCHING

The velocity on a fastball is triggered by **releasing it at the fingertips,** which tells you it should be gripped gently. In fact, you should be able to take the ball from your pitcher's hand without much effort when he's holding it in a fastball grip. No matter which grip is used, Four-Seam or Two, there should be a **finger's worth of distance** between the ball and the palm of the hand. Tell your kids to think of the ball as an egg - treat it as such and everything will work out fine.

For maximum velocity, make sure the **fingers are behind** - not to the side - of the ball when it's released. And that the pressure on the ball is **evenly distributed** between the two fingers.

Curve balls are about **leverage:** Putting enough rotation on the ball so that it can be persuaded to do all those wondrous things that reasoning minds know to be scientifically impossible. What follows is the "How" of throwing a curve ball. You decide the "When".

There are **two ways** to grip the curve ball, one of which is to use the same **Four-Seam** grip as the fastball. This is easier for some kids, because there's no switching back and forth. The downside is that, because of the rotation this grip provides, with only the short seams rotating horizontally through the air, there's less break on the ball.

OR,

The traditional grip, which involves placing the **middle finger on a long seam.** When the ball is released with a downward motion, this grip allows the long seams to "scoop out" more air, resulting in more break. Unlike the fastball, where both fingers share the load equally, the **middle finger applies pressure** on the curve ball. Experienced young pitchers will find they get even better rotation by placing the middle finger not on top, but against the inside of the seam.

TIP LEVEL | PITCHING

 One way to teach your kids about the pressure being applied by the middle finger on the ball is to have them try "spinning" a few curve balls while having the first finger just dangle off to the side.

 FASTFACT: To the naked eye, curve balls break in a continuous arc from the moment they leave the pitcher's hand. Truth be told, it takes some time for the "scooping" action of seams against air to take effect. Curve balls **actually break only the last 10 - 15 feet** from home plate.

 Curve balls are thrown by applying leverage with the wrist, not the elbow. Teach your kids to cock the wrist, with the palm facing outward, to get maximum rotation on the ball.

 Make sure the movement of the wrist is **downward, not sideways.** Since batters swing horizontally, a curve ball breaking horizontally isn't all that hard to hit. Teach your kids to imagine their fingers moving over the top of the ball as they release it. And to **keep the elbow up.** Remember, curve balls are **all about leverage.** Dropping the elbow takes away much of that leverage by not allowing the pitcher to get on top of the ball.

 At the end of the motion the **palm of the hand** faces upward when throwing a curve ball, as if the pitcher could smack himself in the nose with it.

(continued)

TIP LEVEL | PITCHING

FASTFACT - Multiple Choice Question: Think of the rotation on a curve ball in terms of RPM (Revolutions Per Minute), and guess which is the correct answer: (A) 500 RPM; (B), 1000 RPM; or (C), 2000 RPM. Answer: (C). Major league curve balls spin in the range of 1800 - 2000 RPM, making 15 complete rotations in the half-second journey to home plate. Which tells you something about the stress it can place on young arms.

There's also a **"safe" curve ball grip** that young pitchers can be taught, one that involves almost no wrist or elbow movement at all. Grip the ball in the "V" of the hand, that soft fleshy spot where the thumb and 1st finger meet. Wrap the fingers around the ball, along the arc of the seams. To make this pitch work, kids just have to let the ball **tumble out of the hand,** with a stiff wrist and a firm grip. The movement on the ball is provided by the angle of the hand **coming across the body,** down to the opposite knee, so a good Follow-Through is important.

This pitch, though not often taught, offers young pitchers a number of advantages: **(1)** No stress on the arm; **(2)** It's easy to throw; and, **(3)** Because the ball is held in the back of the hand, it has the action of both a curve ball and a change-up.

There are several different ways to **grip a change-up.** The grip your kids use is less important than remembering what makes the change-up work in the first place: Holding the **ball back in the hand** to slow it down as it's released. Nothing more mysterious than that.

The "Circle Change" is easy to teach, and there's a variation you can use for kids with smaller hands:

TIP LEVEL | PITCHING

Have your kids **make a circle** with the **thumb and 1st finger,** then use that circle to secure the ball against the palm of the hand. As with any change-up, the pressure on the ball is provided by the **middle knuckles,** not by the fingertips as with the fastball. The release is with a stiff wrist. Tell your kids to imagine they're using a paint brush or pulling down a window shade. **Leading with the elbow,** keeping it in front of the wrist as the arm comes forward, is another way to throw the pitch.

For kids whose hands aren't quite big enough to make a circle, teach them "the **"Triangle Change"** instead, by extending the thumb and 1st finger straight out, forming a three-sided shape created by the fingers and the base of the hand.

To be effective, any off-speed pitch has to be "sold" - you have to fool the batter into thinking a fastball is on the way. Changing the motion takes away that element of surprise. Make sure that both the motion and the **arm speed** on a change-up are the same as for a fastball. Remember, it's **the grip that slows the ball down.**

It's especially important kids execute a **complete** Follow-Through on any off-speed pitch **- curve ball or change-up -** to help make sure the ball stays down in the strike zone. Slow stuff that stays up in the strike zone is not called an **"Off-Speed Pitch".** It's called an **"Extra Base Hit".**

Some kids pitch in leagues that allow runners to lead off. Learning to pitch from the "Stretch" isn't all that complicated, and here are a few things your kids should know:

(continued)

TIP LEVEL	PITCHING

Pitching from the Stretch is easier for some kids, just because there's less to do. Something to keep in mind as a temporary solution when your kids can't throw strikes. But as for holding runners on, one of the first things to teach your kids is something called the **Slide Step.** This is a quick, shortened drive with the front leg - no high kick, no pause at the Balance Point. It's also the motion of choice when throwing a Pitch-Out.

Using a Slide Step also suggests throwing only fastballs. The leverage needed to break off a good curve ball is harder to come by with a shortened stride. And, if you think the runner's going to steal, there's no reason to throw anything but a fastball.

A good rule for young pitchers to remember is **"First Move, Worst Move".** Teach them not to use their best pick-off move the first time they go after a runner. Use a slower, more exaggerated move to see how the runner reacts and to give him a false sense of confidence. Then nail him with the good one. And never use the same move twice in a row.

Never let the runner have what's called a **"Walking Lead",** where he's allowed to continue moving toward the next base. Most bases are stolen on the pitcher, not on the catcher, and a Walking Lead is a stolen base waiting to happen, because it gives the runner momentum toward the next base. Make the runner stop. Make him respect the move. Give the catcher a fighting chance.

Something right-handed pitchers can do is open the left shoulder, angling it just a bit toward first base, to help them see the runner more clearly and quicken the move over there. Something else they can do is keep the hands higher in the "Set" position to help them get rid of the ball faster.

TIP LEVEL | PITCHING

FastFact: Major league scouts time pitchers to see just how quickly they can get the ball to home plate from the stretch position. Magic number: 1.6 seconds.

The Rule Book says the first motion a pitcher makes has to be in the direction of first base - anything else is a balk. This does allow right-handers to make a Pick-Off move by turning with the pivot foot still inside the mound, instead of stepping back from it.

For left-handers, the move to 1st base is a simple matter of geometry. There's a 90-degree angle connecting home plate, the mound and 1st base. Divide that in half and you get two 45-degree angles. A left-hander's foot has to land in the 45-degree angle closest to 1st base. If he lands in the angle closest to home plate, it's a balk. If his leg goes behind the line connecting the mound and 1st base, it's a balk.

Once the pitcher has come to the "Set" position, meaning the hands have come together and are still, the only part of the body that can move is the head. Even a little wiggle with the hands, shoulders or knees, and the umpire's going to call a balk. Separate the hands and it's a balk. Come to a 2nd "Set" position and it's a balk. Tell your kids when they feel a balk coming to just break contact with the rubber by stepping back from it, take a moment to collect themselves, and try again.

When throwing to 2nd, the quickest move is by turning toward the glove-hand side. That's counter-clockwise for right-handers, clockwise for left-handers.

(continued)

TIP LEVEL	PITCHING

 When attempting a pick-off at either 2nd or 3rd, the pitcher **doesn't have to throw** the ball, just as long as the pivot foot breaks contract with the rubber. Faking a throw to any base with the foot **still in contact** is a balk.

DRILL | Use a **5-gallon trash can,** set on its side, to give pitchers a target to throw into when teaching them where to aim the pick-off throw. This drill also works great for outfielders learning how to make the low throw. Only, you may want to give them a break by providing a larger trash can.

There's a whole series of nifty **pick-off moves** that will serve your kids well and you'll find them in the **Section on Coaching/Game Strategies.**

Maybe the **last thing you teach your kids** about pitching is the **first thing they should remember:** If they learn to throw one kind of pitch consistently for strikes, they'll get batters out in Little League. Throw two kinds of pitches for strikes, they'll get them out in high school. Throw three kinds of pitches for strikes, and maybe one day you'll get to sit in the stands and watch them pitch professionally. The absolute, bottom-line, best way to develop young pitchers is to work on one pitch at a time, until they're able to throw it with confidence, no matter the hitter, no matter the count, no matter the situation. Pitching is about **two things:** Mechanics & Attitude. You've taught them the **Mechanics.** Being in command of every pitch and throwing every pitch with a purpose is where the **Attitude** comes in.

AND REMEMBER , IT'S ONLY A GAME...

New Advanced Pitching Section

This section, **New for the 3rd Edition,** is designed to give young pitchers and their families an advanced look at what goes into becoming successful at the high school and college levels, and beyond.

This information was compiled from **interviews, observations and conversations with major league pitchers and pitching coaches, past and present.** It will take you through an entire year's worth of baseball – from off-season workouts, to pre-game warm-ups and more.

There's even a sub-section on how to impress college and major league scouts.

And be sure to look for **Voices from the Hall of Fame,** throughout this section. What we've done is collect the thoughts from three generations of Hall of Fame pitchers, to give you what is truly an insider's perspective on pitching success.

Enjoy…

Impressing the Scouts

In talking about how to impress college or major league scouts, the first thing to understand is that their process of **evaluation doesn't begin when you take the mound, it begins the moment you take the field.**

In addition to the usual wish list items such as preferred height, weight and MPH on the radar gun, scouts are looking for enthusiasm, command, confidence, leadership qualities, aggressiveness and perhaps above all else, signs that you are a team player.

These are the constants by which you'll be judged. While some scouts prefer tall pitchers, based on the belief that height adds leverage to a pitcher's delivery, others focus more on mechanics and good work habits, because shorter pitchers often have fewer mechanical problems with their delivery.

So, if you're not 6:4 and 220 lbs., don't be discouraged. Focus instead on **who you are and what you do well.**

That said, here's some more of what scouts are looking for:

Velocity & Movement – Extra pop on the fastball and good natural movement are always going to attract a lot of attention.

Arm Angle – Most scouts favor young pitchers with either overhand or three-quarter delivery, rather than sidearm.

The Radar Gun – Although the ability to throw strikes and movement on the fastball are always going to be indicators of future success, because the level of competition in high school can vary so much, many scouts begin by looking for fastballs in the mid-80s or higher.

For left handers, velocity is often less important than movement on the ball and an assortment of good breaking pitches; while for right handers, velocity is often more of a true beginning point

Voices from the Hall of Fame

> *"I'll give the hitter half the plate and he'll give me half the plate in return. But I decide which half is mine."*
>
> – Don Drysdale

Temperament – This is among the intangibles scouts look for. Most kids look, act and feel good, when the going's good. But how do you respond to adversity – walks, errors and the like - whether it's your own making or that of a teammate?

Responsiveness – How do you react when the coach comes to the mound for a visit? Do you listen and respond positively? Or, do you look away and not pay as much attention?

Hustle – As we mentioned earlier, scouts look at you from the moment you walk on the field, so be sure to hustle all the time.

Don't Sweat the Radar Gun – The major leagues, not to mention the Baseball Hall of Fame, are filled with pitchers who made their mark despite below average readings on the radar gun. Knowing how to get batters out is the ultimate recommendation

Keep Calm – During those occasional bad outings, be sure you maintain the same level of poise and confidence at all times. Remember, character counts. In baseball, as in life itself.

Look Them in the Eye – Whether it's a coach, or if you're fortunate enough, a scout who approaches you, be sure to always look him in the eye. It's a sign of confidence and above all, a willingness to accept advice and do whatever it takes to get better.

Confidence, Confidence, Confidence – In the eternal struggle between pitcher and hitter, it's the one who goes into battle believing he's going to win, who usually does.

Mastering the Front Door Fastball

Listen to any game broadcast on TV and you'll hear a lot about "back door curveballs", breaking pitches that cross the front edge of home plate outside the strike zone, but curve in over the side or back edge, for a strike.

Voices from the Hall of Fame

> *"A pitcher has to know he can go to a certain location and be confident the hitter won't be able to take a full swing, when he does. If a pitcher throws a fastball away and the hitter flips it over the second baseman's head for a bloop base hit, it's no big deal.*
>
> *"But if the hitter drives the ball for an extra-base hit to right-center, the pitcher has a problem."*
>
> *– Don Drysdale*

But because it's important for young pitchers to **master the fastball before the breaking ball,** here are some ways you can learn the "Front Door Fastball", a pitch made popular by Greg Maddux and others.

The front door fastball is a two-seam fastball, usually thrown to left handed hitters, that starts as a ball but backs up to catch the inside corner of the plate.

Many hitters, whether they're left handed or right handed, will give up on the pitch early and get caught looking for a called strike. And for left handers in particular, it can be a very difficult pitch to hit fair.

The location of the Front Door Fastball is important, but how you set it up can be even more important. Many pitchers at the major league level attempt to **pitch inside early in the count,** by establishing the fastball just under the hitter's hands. Note that many pitchers will choose a four-seam fastball to accomplish this, because the four-seam fastball is likely to stay straighter and be easier to throw to a certain spot.

As a result, the hitter is being programmed to think of inside fastballs as balls. And that's how you set the hitter up for the front door fastball, the one that breaks back across the inside of the plate.

Voices from the Hall of Fame -

"I was able to blow people away in high school, but as soon as I got to A ball, I wasn't able to do that anymore. I finally realized that you can blow the ball by somebody once, but you're probably not going to do it two or three times in a row."

— Greg Maddux

Key in throwing this pitch, as in all pitches, is stepping where you throw. Here's another key, making sure you have the good balance required to get the kind of movement and control on the pitch that you want.

One tip early on: If you find you're having difficulty getting the ball to move back inside, have somebody check your delivery to see whether you're throwing across your body.

Throwing across your body – meaning that you're landing in a slightly closed position (with the plant foot to your throwing arm side of your back foot) – is a guaranteed way to flatten out your pitches.

Two quick remedies for throwing across your body: 1) Shorten up the arc of your arm; 2) Speed up the arm motion.

To tell whether you might be a good candidate to develop the Front Door fastball, ask yourself this question: "Does my two-seam fastball have a lot of natural movement"?

Another way of telling is by checking your stride step. As just mentioned, to get good movement it's important to step directly at your target. Correcting that is sometimes as simple as pointing your toes to the target corner of home plate.

Stepping to your target lets your body open up at the proper time. It also lets you stay "behind the ball", as opposed to letting your body drift to either side.

Voices from the Hall of Fame –

"I always feel that if you do everything mechanically correct, it's impossible not to throw the ball where you're trying to throw it. If you're consistent with your mechanics, you'll be consistent with your delivery. And ultimately, you're going to be more consistent throwing strikes or at least throwing the ball where you want to throw it."

– Greg Maddux

As to your grip, it's important that your fingers stay on top of the ball. Make sure you don't either lower your arm angle or drop your wrist, in an attempt to get that extra movement. Doing either will produce just the opposite effect.

And, two-seam fastballs that do not move are really not called "two-seam fastballs". They're called "extra base hits".

Don't try to overthrow this pitch. That, too, will result in less movement and just as likely, less control. It's OK to throw it with a bit less velocity, as well.

Be sure to finish your delivery squared up to home plate. A square finish is the result of a balanced delivery and proper follow through.

As you reach the balance point in your delivery and begin to move toward home plate, concentrate on bringing your throwing side hip around firmly, so that you finish squared up. A lazy hip is one more way to make sure the result is throwing across your body.

Remember that the Front Door Fastball is a pitch based entirely on movement and location. Velocity is much less a consideration for success.

Remember, too, that the Front Door Fastball is a psychological weapon as well. It's designed to make the hitter think about the inside corner and to increase your ability to establish dominance.

Voices from the Hall of Fame –

> *"When I see kids throw, a lot of times they're doing too much with their mechanics. I want to try to calm them down. Their head is moving all over the place, they're stepping back too far, they're kicking their leg up too high, they're long arming the ball.*
>
> *"It seems they want to do as much as they can with their mechanics. It should be the other way around. You should do the least amount you have to."*
>
> *—Greg Maddux*

Taking a small Step toward BIG Success

In the old days (that means anytime from the day your dad stopped playing, back to the beginning of recorded history), conventional wisdom was for young pitchers to begin the pitching motion with a big step backward.

Maybe you've seen newsreels of old-time pitchers like Walter Johnson who used a windmill motion: Big back step – High leg kick - Straight over the top delivery - Upright follow through.

But as they say, that was then, this is now.

Today, most effective pitchers are much more economical in their deliveries. They start small and stay compact.

Understand that the back step a pitcher takes to begin the windup is only to allow for a transfer of the weight from the stride or plant foot to the pivot or back foot. Once the weight shift is complete, the pitcher then rotates his hips to get to his balance point.

Voices from the Hall of Fame –

"Confidence is the most important element in a young pitcher's preparation to pitch. Confidence in his ability and in his team's ability. You get confidence by finding where you're comfortable.

"To pitch effectively, a pitcher must repeat the same motion over and over. But you can't do it at 100% effort, all the time.

– Sandy Koufax

Taking a small back step – or as is often done these days, a 45-degree step to the side – takes away the problem of the transfer of weight.

And just the opposite, a long stride back, almost always throws the pitcher off balance, which leaves him trying to compensate for that loss of balance by trying to regain it as quickly as possible. That usually happens around the balance point part of the delivery.

Another thing a long back step does is force the pitcher to move his head – another No, No.

The short back step keeps the head still, but without affecting pitch velocity.

Pitching in Cold Weather

Here are some tips to help make sure that when you are forced to pitch in cold weather, especially at the beginning of the season, you do your arm no harm.

Take extra time with warm up. Get your heart pumping with some running or other aerobic exercise, before you begin to throw.

Cold weather can make it harder to feel the ball with your fingers. If you can't feel the ball as you normally would in warm weather, don't expect to get it until you're partway through the game. But it will come. So don't wear yourself out – or worse, cause injury your arm – in warm up by trying to throw extra in hopes of getting the feeling back.

Make sure you have access to a rosin bag and use it often. You've probably seen early or late season games on TV, when the pitcher will motion to the umpire with his fingers toward his mouth, in essence checking to make sure he can put some extra saliva on his fingers and then transfer that to the rosin bag for extra tackiness that helps improve his grip.

And remember that cold weather is the hitter's problem, too.
The last thing he wants to do is swing at an inside fastball that's sure to send shivers up his arm when he makes contact.

Voices from the Hall of Fame -

> "I would repeat a checklist of things to myself...I ride on my front foot. I want to feel I'm gliding toward home plate... I like to feel the ball snap off my fingertips... I rest my chin against my shoulder until I have to open up... I like to make my back side force my front side out of the way, and then I pull with my front side.
>
> "I like to feel my wrist on top of the ball throughout my delivery. And I make sure I reach my balance point before I move to the plate."
>
> — Tom Seaver

So take control of the inside of the plate, even more than you would in warm weather.

Keeping Young Arms Healthy

Common belief of pitching coaches and physicians who treat athletic injuries is that of the many reasons for arm problems with young pitchers - overuse, poor conditioning, lack of recovery time, among them **– poor mechanics may be the biggest culprit of all.**

Simply said, the human body was not designed to throw a ball overhand. It is a very fatiguing and stressful activity.

In throwing a baseball correctly, the muscles, tendons and ligaments in the arm all have to work together to stabilize and control the body's movements in an effort to reduce the stress being applied.

Voices from the Hall of Fame –

> *"Early on, I simplified my delivery into four basic areas: Small back step, small leg kick, head still, and release the ball from the same angle every time.*
>
> *"I know if I break my hands sooner, it will help me get on top quicker. If my ball is up, I know that's I'm breaking my hands too late. If I break my hands quicker, the ball will come down."*
>
> —Greg Maddux

That's why experienced pitchers know to use the lower body, transferring stress to the larger muscles in the hips and legs. Pitchers who throw with consistent velocity and consistent mechanics use their lower body to help prevent injury.

Here are some stress points different pitches place on the body and as a result, important things to watch out for.

Fastball – When throwing the fastball the greatest amount of velocity is generated by the position of the hand and arm. It's also true that when throwing the fastball more stress is placed on the shoulder and muscles of the upper arm than with other pitches.

With the fastball, unnecessary stress is caused by:

Front shoulder flying open too early.

Stride leg and lower body overly closed at the landing point (throwing across the body).

Improper balance, caused by the upper body tilting away from the target.

Improper weight transfer, caused when the motion is rushed.

Improper position of the hand and elbow, causing a "Stiff arm" motion.

Poor arm slot, meaning the arm is too close to the head, making for an unnatural overhand motion. The opposite can be true as well, with stress caused by the arm being too far away from the body.

Voices from the Hall of Fame –

"Confidence is something you learn in practice. Then in the game, you throw harder as your confidence increases. Early in the game, it might be 90% effort. Later in the game it might be 95 to 98%, as your timing improves."

— Sandy Koufax

Curveball – With the curveball, less stress is placed on the shoulder and more stress is placed on the elbow The hand and arm speed are slower with the curveball as well. With the curveball, the arm angle is often closer to the head, in an effort to get more torque or rotation on the ball.

With the curveball, unnecessary stress is caused by:

Bad position of the hand and wrist, with the palm facing the head.

Improper flexing of the wrist, which in turn causes more compression forces on the elbow.

Trying to throw a directly overhand, or 12-6 (hands on the clock) curveball.

Too wide an arm angle, in effect "Frisbeeing" the ball, which causes more stress on the elbow.

Off-Season Workouts

The goal of any off-season workout program is measured in several ways: One, to help you get stronger for the upcoming season; two, to give you that edge over the other guys when the next season begins.

The third reason is just as important, but often overlooked:

To keep you "in the game", mentally as well as physically.

Realizing the importance of the other factors in your life – school, family, friends, maybe even a part-time job – the best way to make sure your commitment to an off season workout program stays strong is by carving out time for it, putting in on your calendar as you would any other important business and sticking to the routine.

Consistency is the key.

Voices from the Hall of Fame –

"When I was coaching at the University of South Florida, I used a simple drill to determine the natural delivery of my pitchers. I'd get them all out to shortstop, hit them some easy grounders and ask them to throw to first base.

"Although the throw may wind up different, from time to time, each pitcher would make that throw using his natural delivery. Sometimes the problem would be when they took the mound, they'd use more mechanics than they did when throwing naturally from shortstop."

– Robin Roberts

Set a target of two workouts per week, which means you'll have 3-4 days off in between, throughout the entire off-season. The other days are set aside for running.

Begin your off-season routine by stretching. Remember, the muscle groups you used during the season tend to go to sleep when not used regularly. **A good ten-minute stretch before you begin to throw will help wake them up.**

That ten-minute stretch should include slow movements, with full range of motion, especially with your throwing arm and shoulder.

When it's time to throw, start off at a limited distance, no more than 40 feet at first, then increase the length of your throws in 20-foot increments - going to 80, then 100 and then 120 feet. But do it gradually. **NO LONG TOSS RIGHT AWAY,** especially if you haven't thrown in recent weeks before you begin your off-season program.

Mimic the last half of your throwing motion as you do, in effect as if you were pitching out of a stretch position with runners on base. This will help with that muscle memory.

Take **between 5 and 10 throws at each distance,** before going on to the next. But a cautionary note: **If you feel any discomfort, whether it's even a slight muscle pull, back down to the previous distance. If that doesn't make the discomfort go away, stop the workout altogether and find out the reason for the pain.**

No reason, whatsoever, to go into the upcoming season with arm problems.

Once you've reached the distance you feel is your limit (and remember, taking 5 – 10 throws at each previous distance before you max out), reverse the program. But this time, take only 2-3 throws eat each distance until you're back to where you began, at 40 feet.

Small point, but one to remember: Always use the four-seam grip when throwing in your off-season program.

And if bad weather becomes a problem, find a place indoors to throw, rather than take the time off and expect to come back in the same level of progress you enjoyed before the bad weather hit.

AND DON'T FORGET YOUR RUNNING, TOO....

In-Season Workout Program

Most professional scouts look to the amount of work a young pitcher has thrown during the season, as a benchmark of how many "arrows" he has left when the season ends.

And for most scouts, the math is very simple: **The age of the pitcher x 10 = The maximum number of innings per season.**

Voices from the Hall of Fame –

> *"When a pitcher is cruising along and then suddenly loses it, it's usually because his rhythm goes out. For some reason, his inner clock fouled up and he's not there physically any more.*
>
> *"When that happens, he needs to slow down and get mentally together after each pitch. Go back to your keys. My key was my right hip. I wanted to see how far I could move my right hip toward home plate before anything else happened.*
>
> *"But remember, it's different for everybody."*
>
> *– Sandy Koufax*

That number includes winter ball, pre-season and regular season games, but not the in-season workout program.

Presuming that you pitch in no more than two games per week, and a distance of 4-5 days between games, here's an in-season program designed to keep you strong and healthy for the entire season.

Day 1 After a Game –

30-pitch Warm-Up Routine – NO LONG TOSS.

Day 2 After –

30-Pitch Warm-Up Routine, followed by a 24 to 36-pitch bullpen routine.

Day 3 After –

30-Pitch Warm-up Routine, followed by a 20-pitch bullpen routine.

Day 4 After –

30-Pitch Warm Up Routine, LONG TOSS AN OPTION, but no more than 80 feet.

Most of the throwing done as part of the warm-up routine should be done on flat ground, rather than off the mound. Flat ground throwing is less stressful on young arms.

Another way to measure your routine is by minutes spent, as opposed to by pitches thrown. This is a matter of individual choice, but one made in consultation with your coach and, of course, your parents.

Voices from the Hall of Fame –

> "But there's a thousand ways to pitch. You just have to find the way that works best for you. As far as mechanics go, whatever you do naturally is usually the best thing to do.
>
> "And I always make it a practice to relearn my mechanics during the game. Although you can get a good sense of how well you're doing from the bullpen warm-ups, until you get into the game, that's when you really start to learn and mature as a pitcher."
>
> — Greg Maddux

If you choose the minutes thrown version, here's an outline for that, as well.

Long Toss -

4 Minutes @ 40 feet. – No Wind Up. Emphasis on closed front side and follow through.

3 Minutes @ 60 feet – Wind Up. Emphasis on closed front side and follow through.

3 Minutes @ 80 feet – Wind Up. Emphasis on closed front side and follow through.

3 Minutes @ 100 feet – Wind Up. Emphasis on follow through.

2 Minutes @ 120 feet – Wind Up. Emphasis on long arm motion and arm arc.

1 Minute @ 60 feet - Wind Up. Emphasis on staying on top of the ball.

Flat Ground -

Flat ground throwing should be **done at no more than 70% of maximum effort.** The purpose of flat ground throwing is to emphasize certain aspects of the pitching motion.

Flat ground throwing also should be **done at just less than regular pitching** distance, meaning if you're in high school and throwing at 60 feet, mound to home plate, then do your flat ground work at 55 feet or so.

Sample Checkpoints:
1. Set position
2. Balance point (top of delivery)
3. Ball-Glove separation
4. Follow Through (Loose arm out front

Sample Pitch Schedule – Wind Up:
1. 5 Fastballs
2. 5 Change ups
3. 5 Breaking Balls (If part of normal repertoire)

Sample Pitch Schedule – Stretch Position:
1. 5 Fastballs
2. 5 Change ups
3. 5 Breaking balls (If part of normal repertoire)

On game days, it can be stretching, followed by 1/2 of usual warm up routine, followed by 40 to 50-pitch bullpen routine.

Game Day Warm Up Routine

The mission of a game-day warm up routine is very simple:
To get the arm and body working as one unit.

The pre game warm up is in many respects the most important part of a pitcher's routine on game day. Most injuries occur not during the game, but during warm ups.

Foul Line Throws -

Start your game day warm up routine along the foul line. Do your stretches. Do some running, as well.

While throwing from the foul line, **throw in increments of no more than six pitches per sequence, throwing at an increasingly greater distance with each sequence.** Then back down to the distance at which you began. In effect, this part of the game day routine is very similar to the routine you went through in the off season.

Voices from the Hall of Fame –

> *"I'd pitch my way out of slumps by throwing batting practice without a protective screen. It wouldn't be like just throwing on the side, because there is a hitter up there. In BP, you have no worries. Your goal is to throw strikes and let the batter hit it.*
>
> *"With the screen gone, you have to be ready to field a ball hit back to you."*
>
> *– Sandy Koufax*

Bullpen Throws -

Experienced pitchers know that the goal of bullpen warm up before the game is to get into a zone of comfort, then trying to take as much of that zone with them to the mound.

The first phase of bullpen warm up before the game is to work on getting the ball down as much as possible. Hit the catcher's target low in the strike zone consistently, before working side to side.

Warm Up Sequence -

1. Fastballs (9 Pitches)
    a. 3 Middle of the plate (Emphasis on low strikes)
    b. 3 Away
    c. 3 In

2. Change-ups (7 Pitches)
    a. 3 Middle Down
    b. 1 Fastball Away
    c. 3 Middle Down

3. Breaking Balls (8 Pitches – If part of normal repertoire)
    a. 3 With Catcher Standing up in Front of Home Plate
    b. 1 Fastball down the Middle
    c. 1 Fastball Away
    d. 3 Breaking Balls for Strikes

4. Repeat Sequences 1-3 from Stretch Position (If applicable)

5. New Sequence Mix (8 Pitches)
    a. 2 Fastballs away
    b. 2 Breaking Balls
    c. 2 Fastballs (2-Seam if part of repertoire)
    b. 2 Change ups (Low, Down the Middle)

6. Pitch-Outs (2 Pitches)
    a. 1 to Left Side
    b. 1 to Right Side

7. Fastball (1 Pitch)

Some pitchers like to work fast, others like to work slow, so it's important that this pre game warm up routine be no more than 12 minutes and/or 45 pitches in length, if no pitching from the stretch position is done, or 80 pitches in length if pitching from the stretch is included.

But on game days especially, find out what combination of routines works for you and stick with it.

Scouting From the Bench

Whether you're scheduled to pitch that day or not, some of the most valuable work you will ever do will be in "scouting" the opposition from your own bench.

Remember, though, that **just as you can gain insight into the opposing hitters, they can gain insight into you.**

For example, how often do you throw a fastball when you're behind in the count? If you don't mix n something other than the fastball even once in a while, chances are very good they're going to be looking for one.

Voices from the Hall of Fame –

> "The first thing I had to learn about throwing two-seam fastballs inside to left handed hitters is that I have to step there. You're pretty much going to throw the ball where you step.
>
> "If you want to throw the ball away to a right handed hitter, you step away. If you want to throw it in, you step in. It's almost like if I'm going to throw to the right field foul pole, I'll step there."
>
> — Greg Maddux

How often does your catcher begin his signs with the fastball sign? If your catcher is in the habit of putting down one finger (fastball) first, then you can be tipping your pitches simply by the number of times you shake your head (1 time means a curve is coming; 2 times, a change up is coming, etc.)

Getting back to scouting the opposition, **understand that most – perhaps all – hitters are basically fastball hitters.** That's the pitch they're looking for; that's the pitch they want to drive.

To tell how good a fastball hitter a hitter is, check the first swing he takes on the fastball. Even if he fouls it off – especially if he fouls it straight back – the kind of swing he takes can be an indication he's quick enough to get around on the fastball.

Also check the hitter's front foot. That's often a giveaway as to where he wants to hit the ball. A right handed batter whose front foot lands toward the left field line is looking to pull the ball. When the front foot lands toward the first base line, he's looking to hit the ball the other way. Opposite rules apply, of course, for left handed hitters.

Hands held high usually indicate a low ball hitter, while short, stocky hitters usually like the ball up in the strike zone.

A lot can be learned even in warm ups. For example, which players take the lead in stretching exercises? **Chances are,** they're the best players, too.

If you watch batting practice, which hitters hit first and which ones hit last? Chances are the better hitters hit earlier in the batting practice, while the others hit later on.

Try to identify the power hitters, the pull hitters, the contact hitters, the bunters and any other identifications you can make.

It's also possible to categorize hitters by their stance:

The Plate Crowder –
A guy who stands close to the plate is usually a good fastball hitter. If he crowds the plate AND moves up in the box, chances are he's not a good breaking ball hitter.

Pitch this type of hitter down in the strike zone. Don't make the mistake of throwing him all fastballs, because that's what he's probably looking for. If you pitch him inside, make sure you get it far enough inside that he can't drive he ball. Slow curves also can be effective.

But above all else, stay aggressive. The easiest way to turn a good hitter into a great hitter is by pitching defensively.

The Diver –

This is the type of hitter who stands away from the plate and deep in the box. He likes the ball away because he likes to get his arms extended. Hitters like these often have longer, slower swings as well.

Since he's aggressive in moving toward the plate, opening his hips early as he does, **he will try to pull most pitches.**

If the Diver is a lefty, he's going to like the ball down in the strike zone. The good news for you is that he'll usually have difficulty keeping pitches thrown inside from hooking foul.

If he's right handed, he's probably more of a high ball hitter, just like most other right handed hitters. Sometimes, he'll even try to tomahawk high pitches well out of the strike zone.

Pitch this guy by getting ahead in the count, then try to get him to swing at something outside the strike zone. This is known as "expanding the strike zone".

The Diver #2 –

There's another type of "Diver" and that's the one who stands deep in the box and away from the plate, but keeps his hands lower. This type of hitter nearly always has an "inside-out" swing, meaning he's looking to hit the ball the other way. His power is going to be to right center. He likes the ball up in the strike zone and tries to hit a lot of line drives.

Voices from the Hall of Fame –

> *"The art of pitching is the art of instilling fear."*
>
> *– Sandy Koufax*

Since he likes the ball up, try to pitch Diver #2 down in the strike zone. If you go inside, stay around the knees since a low inside pitch is almost impossible to hit to the opposite field.

When you pitch him away, do it with off-speed stuff, making him supply his own power.

The Puller –

This type of hitter usually stands back in the box, but keeps his hands higher than other types of hitters. Like Diver #1, he likes to extend his arms but often steps in the bucket. He's likely to be a low ball hitter with power and be very aggressive.

Get him out with fastballs up in the strike zone and change ups down, although a fastball down and away will often result in an easy ground ball to the opposite field.

You'll be making a mistake by throwing fastballs thigh high, on the inside half of the plate. If you try to get him out with a change-up BE SURE you don't tip it off by changing your motion – either dropping your arm angle or slowing your motion. Either of those mistakes just gives him more advance notice of something slow that he can drive.

Switch Hitter –

Most switch hitters are right handed by nature, then learn to hit from the left side. Most are also spray hitters, hitting the ball to all fields.

Pitch him by keeping the ball down and away, until he proves he can hit it the other way with power. Throw something soft on the outside corner, as your out pitch. But be wary of curveballs. One reason most switch hitters like to switch hit is to take away the effectiveness of the curveball.

Last, understand that off speed pitches – breaking balls in particular – will remain an advantage for you if you locate them. **Good off speed pitches are rarely ever hit hard. While bad ones – ones up in the strike zone in particular – are often crushed.**

And most of all, stay with your strength. Don't analyze too much. Just use these tips to gain some leverage in the battle with the hitters.

NO MATTER WHICH TYPE OF HITTER YOU'RE FACING, DON'T GET BEAT WITH ANYTHING LESS THAN YOUR BEST PITCH....

Voices from the Hall of Fame –

> *"If you're standing by the side of the freeway and one car goes by at 65 miles per hour and the next one goes by a 67 miles per hour, you can't tell the difference.*
>
> *"That's why I change speeds all the time."*
>
> *– Greg Maddux*

20 Rules for Sizing Up the Hitter

1. Tall hitters like the ball down.

2. Short hitters like the ball up

3. Left-handed hitters like the ball down, (except when facing left handed pitchers, then they like the ball up).

4. Hitters with wide stances are contact hitters and like the ball up. They also don't strike out much.

5. Most hitters are fastball hitters and will swing at the first fastball they see.

6. Most switch hitters are natural right hand hitters and have more power from the right side.

7. Hitters with "inside-out" swings like the ball middle-in.

8. Pull hitters will chase inside breaking balls.

9. Hitters who hold the bat straight up are low ball hitters.

10. Hitters who hold the bat flat are high ball hitters.

11. Most hitters will take the first curveball they see.

12. Most power hitters, especially, don't want to waste an at bat by chasing a slow breaking pitch.

13. Hitters with long strides are easier to get out with change ups.

14. Hitters who have "hitches" in their swings can be jammed with pitches just under the hands.

15. The way a hitter reacts to the first fastball he sees indicates how good a fastball hitter he is.

16. Don't ever speed up a hitter's bat by throwing him off speed stuff when he's yet to prove he can hit the fastball.

17. Just because a hitter hits a bad curveball hard somewhere doesn't mean he can hit a good curveball.

18. There's a point when you can become too aggressive. Throwing only

    fastballs just because you're afraid to walk a batter can turn a good hitter into a great hitter. Pitch aggressively, but mix up your pitches when you do.

19. Always believe that the best you have can beat the best he has. Stick with your strengths.

20. Make the hitter hit your pitch. Remember, even the best of them fail two out of every three times at bat.

When Bad Things Happen to Good Pitchers

Every pitcher who ever lived, lived with the knowledge that one of every four, five or six trips to the mound, it just wasn't going to be his day.

Other than injury, most of those occasions can be traced to temporary breakdowns in mechanics. Here's a checklist you can use, to find the problem and fix it.

Set-Up –

1. Feet slightly spread on throwing side of pitching rubber (third base side for right handers, first base side for lefties).

2. Body weight over stride (front) leg.

3. Torso upright.

4. Hips and shoulders square to home plate.

1st Movement –

1. Short drop step, either straight back or at 45-degree angle.

2. Pivot foot lands inside – not on top – of pitching rubber.

3. Hands lift above head.

4. Back of glove toward hitter.

5. Torso still upright.

6. View of ball obscured from hitter and base coaches.

Balance Point –

1. Hands move down to middle of torso (stomach area).

2. Hands lift to highest position, at or above beltline.

3. Torso erect, not tilted backward or to either side.

4. Hips and shoulders turned.

5. Eyes remain parallel to ground.

6. Head remains still and over back leg.

Separation and Stride —

1. Separation of hands occurs simultaneously with beginning of stride.

2. Back of glove higher than elbow when rotating to face catcher.

3. Front shoulder moves directly toward catcher.

4. Throwing arm moves down, back and up toward second base
    in easy manner.

5. Throwing hand moves palms down until completion of back swing,
    then up toward shoulder height.

6. Lead arm moves to shoulder height simultaneously with back swing.

7. Stride is directly toward catcher's target.

8. Stride foot lands in same spot, each time.

Acceleration —

1. Eyes remain parallel to ground.

2. Torso remains erect.

3. Throwing elbow higher than throwing shoulder.

4. Fingers on top of the ball.

5. Wrist behind the ball.

Deceleration —

1. Weight transfer continues through release point.

2. Pivot foot heel rotates out and up.

3. Throwing shoulder pointed at catcher's target.

4. Pivot foot lands even with plant foot, for proper fielding position.

> *"I liked throwing off the mound best, but long toss if OK as long as you don't change your mechanics by trying to throw too far.*
>
> *"Dodger catchers always sat on the outside corner when I pitched. When I came inside, I threw to the inside corner of the pate. I tried to block out the hitter. He is never a target."*
>
> — *Sandy Koufax*

When Good Things Happen to Good Pitchers

The flip side is also true. For those three of every four, or four of every five outings when things do go well, there's a combination of reasons and they also have to do with mechanics.

Here's another list of checkpoints for you to use, to help keep the rhythm of those good outings going.

1. Did I check my defense before making the pitch?

2. Did I take a deep breath and am I in a comfortable position before making the pitch?

3. Is my pivot foot into the "slot" inside the rubber as I begin my delivery?

4. Am I standing in the right spot on the rubber – on the third base side if I'm a right hander, on the first base side if I'm a lefty?

5. Is my weight slightly on my stride leg as I begin?

6. Are my eyes focused on the catcher's target?

7. Is my mind relaxed and concentrating only on getting the batter out?

8. Is my first step back always the same?

9. Is my step back a short one, whether it's straight back or to the side?

10. Did I reach my balance point before continuing the delivery?

11. Is my leg kick at least belt high?

12. If I'm a power pitcher, is my leg kick a bit higher than that?

13. If I'm a control pitcher, is my leg kick a bit lower than that?

14. At my balance point, is my front side shoulder pointing directly toward home plate?

15. At my balance point, is my front side hip pointing directly toward home plate?

16. At my balance point, am I looking directly at the catcher's target?

17. Is my stride foot directly under my knee at my balance point?

18. Does my body come toward home plate in a controlled manner and at a consistent speed?

19. Do my hands break naturally, at a comfortable distance away from my body?

20. Does my stride foot always land in exactly the same spot?

21. Is my arm at its highest point of the arc at the moment my stride foot lands?

22. Are the toes of my stride foot pointed straight at the target when they land?

23. Is my shoulder closed and my glove hand thumb pointed down when my stride foot lands?

24. Is my head still and are my eyes focused when I deliver the ball to home plate?

25. Am I throwing the ball with my body in control, or am I overthrowing?

26. Am I thinking only about hitting the target when I release the ball?

27. Is my follow through smooth and am I in position to field the ball when I throw?

28. In the stretch position, do I use a "slide step" to keep the runner off balance?

29. In the stretch position, do I vary the amount of time I hold the ball in my glove before delivery?

30. Did I "freeze" the runner, making him stop increasing his lead before I delivered the ball?

Work Fast, Throw Strikes

Maybe the most succinct and enduring wisdom ever offered about pitching success was a line attributed to Ray Miller, former Major League pitcher and legendary pitching coach.

"Work fast, throw strikes, and change speeds", was what he said.

Voices from the Hall of Fame –

> *"Between starts, I always liked to throw a lot. My theory was that if I threw too much on the side between starts, I might not get out of the eighth or ninth inning. If I threw too little, I might not get out of the first."*
>
> *– Sandy Koufax*

Work Fast helps keep the defense in the game. Slow down only when you're in trouble. Take a moment to collect yourself, regain your focus and find a way to work through the problems at hand.

Throw Strikes is obvious, but remember there is such a thing as a bad strike, a fastball down the middle or a lazy curveball that spins its way to home plate. Make sure the strikes you throw are good strikes.

Change Speeds is often the hardest thing of this three-part concept for young pitchers to grasp the full meaning of. Because changing speeds doesn't just mean adding change ups to the mix. Changing speeds also means changing the speeds of your fastball and your curveball, too.

Stay on Top

When pitches tend to flatten out, for young pitchers especially, one very common reason is not staying on top of the ball.

But when most young pitchers hear that advice, their first reaction is to elevate their arm angle. Problem is that by elevating the arm angle, it's changing the pitcher's natural motion.

Voices from the Hall of Fame –

> "My final advice to young pitchers is something Warren Spahn said a long time ago, 'The plate is seventeen inches wide. Fifteen inches belong to the hitter. Learn to work the two inches that belong to the pitcher'."
>
> — Sandy Koufax

So know that "Staying on Top" has more to do with the wrist than the arm itself. Consistently effective pitchers know to keep their **wrist pointed upward, the hand behind the ball and the finger over the top.**

So the next time you get in trouble and hear the words "Stay on Top", take a moment to "look" at your pitching motion. Visualize whether the wrist is up, the hand is behind the ball and the fingers are over the top.

Nothing to it…

Working with your Catcher

There is probably no more important relationship in all of sports than that shared by pitcher and catcher. To work for maximum effectiveness, here are some keys to making that relationship work for you.

1. Does your catcher know what your "out" pitch is and when to call it?

2. Do you and your catcher establish a "game plan" before you take the mound?

3. Do you and your catcher stay within your game plan at least 90% of the time?

4. Is your catcher unafraid to call for the inside fastball when it's important to throw it?

5. Does your catcher work both the inside and outside halves of the plate or does he just set up with his target in the middle of the plate on every pitch?

6. Does your catcher work up and down in the strike zone as well?

7. Do you and your pitcher share information from personal "scouting reports" before the game begins?

8. Does your catcher vary the sequence of signs, not always starting out with one finger for the fastball?

9. Do you and your catcher ever use the "fake shake" meaning shaking your head but in actuality agreeing on that pitch, in order to fool the other team?

10. Do you and your catcher understand the difference between "pitching" and "throwing" and does he know the telltale signs when you stop being a "pitcher" and start being a "thrower?"

Final Thoughts

I was fortunate enough to play this game for 15 years; I've spent another 15 teaching my sons, and the sons of others, how to play it as well.

Of my two sons, Christopher and Zachary, Zachary alone stills plays the game. Now in his third year of college, he's a pitcher, like his dad.

Christopher still loves baseball, too, even though it's no longer part of his every day life. It remains, however, an every day part of our relationship.

In writing this **Advanced Pitching Section for the New 3rd Edition,** I wanted to take you and your family through an entire year's worth of what it takes for a pitcher to succeed at the highest levels.

In effect, replicating the experiences I had and those I've been given the opportunity to share with the next generations of young players.

So enjoy…

While I get the chance to sit in the stands and watch Zachary take everything he's learned and put it to good use, every time he takes the mound.

It just doesn't get any better than that.

Don Marsh
Spring, 2004

Chapter 2

Infielding/Outfielding

The tendency for some kids to turn in horror at the sight of an approaching baseball is, to be certain, the product of natural fear triggered by something so hard coming so fast. A basketball player's life is usually free of such self-preservation concerns. Nonetheless, teaching your kids the proper way to catch, as well as throw, a ball should prove an easy enough task, because it is so much a matter of fundamentals. Fundamentals such as these...

The "Baseball Tips" System™:

⚾	Age 10 & Under/Beginner
⚾⚾	Age 12 & Under/Intermediate
⚾⚾⚾	Age 16 & Under/Advanced
DRILLS	Are called out

TIP LEVEL	INFIELDING
⚾	If you believe there can be easy answers to even the most complicated questions, then apply the principle of **"Thumbs & Pinkies"** to teaching your kids how to catch a baseball. It's a simple lesson, and it's told this way: To catch a ball that's above the waist, put the thumbs (bare hand and glove) together. To catch a ball below the waist, put the pinkies together. Now, who says this game's hard to play???
⚾	There's absolutely nothing wrong with using tennis balls instead of baseballs when introducing kids to the concept of Thumbs & Pinkies. Baseball is fun. Baseballs can be very unforgiving.

(continued)

TIP LEVEL	INFIELDING
	"Thumbs & Pinkies" tells your kids **how** to catch a ball, **"Triangle"** tells them **where.** The first side of the Triangle is the imaginary line running between the shoulders, the other two sides made up by the forearms angling together in front of the body. Teach your kids to try and catch every ball in the Triangle, whether it's in the air or on the ground.
	At the tip of the "Triangle" is the glove. In the proper fielding position, the glove should be "Open", with the **palm facing the ball.** This places the surface of the glove perpendicular to the ball and gives kids the best chance of fielding it cleanly.
	If kids were cars, the **elbows** would be a young baseball player's **shock absorbers.** Don't let your kids catch the ball with their elbows against their body, nor with them fully extended. Keeping the elbows slightly bent gives kids the range they need while helping to cushion the impact of the ball.
DRILL	Have your kids "draw" circles in the air with their elbows against their sides. Now make them with the elbows extended. See how much bigger the circles are. **Translation: More range.**
	A quick sketch of the **"Ready Position"** would find that the feet are no less than shoulder-width apart and parallel, the weight is on the balls of the feet, not the heels, the knees are bent, the head is up, and the hands are out in front. Kids with shorter arms may find it's better to **widen their stance** just a bit.
DRILL	The Ready Position is all about center of gravity. For kids, that center of gravity should be somewhere near the mid-pelvis area. Have your kids stand before you,

TIP LEVEL	INFIELDING
DRILL	eyes closed, in the Ready Position. Test them by pulling or pushing them gently, checking to see how well they maintain balance. The more upright they are, the more bent over at the waist instead of at the knees they are, the harder it will be for them to pass the test.
	Kids have a tendency to rest their hands on their knees in the Ready Position. Better they begin with their hands **out in front** of the body, since that's where they'll be catching the ball anyway.
	Teach your kids to **bend more at the knees** than at the waist when fielding a ground ball. Bending at the waist brings the upper body forward, changing the center of gravity and making it harder to maintain balance.
DRILL	The perfect alignment for fielding ground balls also involves having a flat back when the ball comes into the glove. Place a cup of very cold water on your young infielder's back. If the water doesn't spill, the back's flat enough. If it does, just flatten the back more next time.
	Some coaches tell young infielders to keep their glove on the ground. Teach yours to **"Keep the Glove Lower Than the Ball"**, instead. A player's normal instinct is to retract the arms when a ground ball comes, making the glove rise in the process. This is one reason so many ground balls get between so many players' legs. Keep the glove lower than the approaching ball, so that when the arms retract, ball and glove will meet at the same place, at the same time. Just like they're supposed to.
	A by-product of **Keeping the Glove Lower Than the Ball** is how it helps cushion the ball on impact into the glove, creating those "soft hands" baseball scouts love to see infielders possess.

(continued)

TIP LEVEL	INFIELDING

DRILL

Have your kids stand in front of you, in the **Ready Position.** Take a baseball in your hand and raise or lower it in front of them. See how quickly they react, looking to see that the hands are always lower than the ball.

Keeping the Glove Lower Than the Ball begins the process of snaring the elusive grounder. **"Having the Shoulders Squared"** helps close the deal. Shoulders Squared means they are at **right angles** to the path of the ball. Young players have a tendency to catch balls outside the shoulders, or with one farther in front than the other. Almost everything you can possibly teach your kids about catching a baseball won't work if the shoulders aren't squared.

To help kids who have a habit of lifting their head before the ball comes, teach them to **aim the bill of the cap** at the ball, following it all the way into the glove.

An infielder's success is in many ways due more to footwork than arm strength. One of the best ways teach kids the proper **footwork sequence** on ground balls, regardless of which position they play, is with a simple **"Right/Left".** As the ball approaches, teach them to take a short step to the side with the right foot and then a longer step to the side with the left. This helps expand their range and, even more importantly, gives them momentum toward 1st base for the throw that follows.

For your left handed 1st basemen, the proper sequence is, of course, "Left/Right", for fielding the ground ball.

After teaching your kids the footwork sequence we've just talked about, teach them that the ideal place to field the ground ball is just inside the left hip, for right-handers, and just inside the right hip, for lefties.

TIP LEVEL	INFIELDING

Having mastered the "Right/Left" sequence for fielding the balls, teach them to continue, with one more "Right/Left" to gather momentum for the throw to 1st base. These two tips combined - "Right/Left" to field the ball and another "Right/Left" for the throw - will eventually go as far toward perfecting infielding skills as anything else you can do to teach your more advanced kids.

DRILL

There's a great drill that follows the introduction of these two tips. Just have your kids practice these two sequences by calling out, "Right/Left, Right/Left", as they mimic fielding and then throwing the ball. When introducing the drill, call out the sequences slowly, in effect choreographing the exercise without using a baseball. Then go a bit faster, still without using a ball, and finally, by rolling or hitting a ball toward them.

One thing to watch out for, especially if you introduce the drill just mentioned, is to make sure your kids don't "hitch", or bring their hands into their chest, before making the throw. Try to let them know that the way to use this sequence to their best advantage is by turning it into as fluid a motion as possible.

The proper grip for throwing the ball is the Four-Seam, also talked about in the Chapter on Pitching. Teach your kids to grip the ball across the seams, at their widest point. What you'll have is **four fingers all touching a seam.** What makes this the grip of choice is that the ball is released with backwards spin, making it travel farther and straighter. Can't ask for much more than that.

Teach your kids to hold the ball **at the fingertips,** and gently. The harder they grip the ball, the harder it will be

(continued)

TIP LEVEL	INFIELDING

 to control. In fact, you should be able to take the ball from their hand without too much effort. Just tell them the ball is an egg, and should be treated as such.

 Another trick to see that they're holding the ball properly is to have them **place a finger** between the ball and the palm of the hand. If they can't do that, they're holding the ball too far back in the hand.

 After catching the ball with the shoulders squared, the front shoulder rotates all the way forward 90 degrees for the throw, in effect pointing the way to the target. **Closing the Front Shoulder** just might be the most important thing you can teach your kids about throwing the ball because it allows them to use not just the arm, but the lower body as well, by placing their weight over the back leg before the throw. You can always tell when your kids make an "Open Shoulder" throw - it's the one that either bounces three times or sails way over the intended target.

 Just as with the pitching motion, make sure the elbow is at least shoulder-high at the point of release and that the fingers are behind - not to the side - of the ball. And remember the 1 o'clock analogy for the release point, from the chapter on Pitching.

 What we just talked about applies to left-handers as well, but with them the release point is around 11 o'clock.

One of the more difficult things to teach young infielders is when to charge the ground ball and when to sit back. The basic rule of thumb is that it's easier to catch the ground ball as it comes off the grass than after the 1st

TIP LEVEL	INFIELDING

hop on the dirt. Easier, but not always possible. For kids just starting out, it's probably more important they stay true to the idea of catching **every ball in the Triangle,** and leave decisions about charging the ball to future seasons. For more experienced players, the phrase "Don't Wait for the Bad Hop" is a good one to remember.

Maybe the easiest, and best, way to teach your kids about meeting the ball is to let them know that, whenever possible, they want to be **moving toward the grounder** as it approaches. Sometimes, though, being stationary is the best a good infielder can do. Moving backward is a sure sign that an error is on the way.

Maybe the easiest way to teach kids to always be moving toward the ground ball is by having them do **"Creep Steps"** as the pitcher is about to throw the ball. Creep Steps means having them take **small steps** toward the batter, giving them momentum toward home plate and, at the same time, keeping them off their heels.

Following up on the idea of Creep Steps, teach your kids to set up just a bit behind where they actually want to field the ground ball, remembering that, by using the Creep Steps, they'll be cutting the distance between themselves and the batter. An easy way for kids just starting to use this Step is by marking an "X" in the dirt in front of them - the "X" being the spot where the want to be when the ground ball comes - and set up just behind that to leave room for the Steps.

DRILL Have your kids practice setting up by having them mark off that "X" in the dirt and move back just a bit. Call out "Creep Steps" and let see for themselves whether they wind up on that "X" or make adjustments if they don't.

(continued)

TIP LEVEL	INFIELDING

The **Close Step** is something extra you can teach kids accustomed to charging the ball. This is especially good for infielders on the left side (shortstops and 3rd basemen), who are faced with longer throws. Teach these kids not to be so concerned about fielding the ball in the middle of the Triangle and squared up, but to **field it off the right foot, with the left foot forward,** instead. The Close Step allows the left side of the body to automatically turn toward 1st base as the ball is being fielded, making for a quicker throw.

Using a Close Step means fielding the ball **a little closer to the body** than usual. Fielding the ball too far out front while using the Close Step can result in a loss of balance, turning a potential great play into a two-base error.

This does not suggest kids shouldn't approach the ball **Squared Up.** Good infielders act on the belief that there's a bad hop in every ground ball just waiting to happen. Teach them to use the Close Step **only at the last instant.**

One of the other things the Close Step teaches, something that's good for all infielders to remember, is to begin the act of throwing while **coming out of the crouch.** This saves time and helps guarantee an accurate throw, no matter which position they play.

This is one of those small tricks you can teach your kids that will last as long as they play baseball. In fact, should they ever have the opportunity to attend a major league tryout, it's guaranteed one of the things they'll be asked to do is throw from deep short. Using the **Close Step** is a signal that they know how to play the game at a higher level. And that they had a **good teacher** along the way.

TIP LEVEL	INFIELDING
DRILL	Place a row of baseballs in the infield grass and have your kids come in to scoop up the ball, practicing the Close Step. Having a stationary object at first makes it easier for them to concentrate on the footwork. Try this a few times, then rolls some balls, then hit some grounders, making sure they stayed squared while coming in.
	For those plays when the ball has to be scooped up **barehanded,** teach your kids to reach for the backside of the ball. Since the body's moving forward at the time, reaching for the top often results in missing the ball or not gripping it securely enough to make a good throw.
	There are two other steps infielders should be taught: **The Shuffle** and the **Crossover.** Shuffle Steps are easy to teach, something along the lines of walking like a crab. Just remember that the **feet should never come together** on the Shuffle Step. The good thing about them is that they help kids maintain balance - the bad thing is that they provide only limited range. Which brings us to the **Crossover:**
	Crossover Steps (left-over-right, or right-over-left) allow kids to cover ground in a hurry. Just make sure they **stay bent at the waist** while doing the Crossover. Standing up and then bending down to field the ball is a sure-fire way to mess up the play. Same for Shuffle Steps, too.
DRILL	To help practice **Shuffles and Crossovers,** have your kids stand side-by-side, about ten feet apart. Stand in front of them and use your arms to signal which kind of step you want them to execute: Left arm away from your body means Crossover to that side. Left arm down means Shuffle to that side. Right arm away, Crossover to that side. Right arm down, Shuffle to that side. Make sure they stay bent at the waist and at the knees, no matter which step they take, no matter which direction they go.

(continued)

TIP LEVEL	INFIELDING

1st base is one of several places on the baseball field where left-handers have a decided advantage - the others being right field, the pitcher's mound, and the batter's box. Being left-handed allows the 1st baseman, whose glove is on the right hand, to be more effective fielding balls to his right, where most of the action will be. It also allows him to face the infield when taking throws.

There's one job requirement unique to the 1st base position: The ability to dig balls out of the dirt. 1st basemen don't need strong arms; they do need good hand-eye coordination.

The other part of being a good 1st baseman has to do with footwork. Teach your kids **never to anchor the foot** to the bag before the throw comes. Anchoring too soon and stretching for a ball that's yet to be thrown makes it difficult to react if it's off-target. Tell them to work the **corners of the bag,** staying nearby, knowing where the bag is without looking down, and making contact only when the ball's on the way.

Teach your 1st basemen to use the corner nearest the plate on throws from 3rd or short and the one nearest right field on throws from 2nd. Never stand on **top of the bag.** Besides not being as close to the throw as possible, there's also the danger of being spiked by an oncoming runner who's concentrating only on the bag, and not on any exposed ankles or feet. When holding runners on, anchor the right foot to the home plate side of the bag and use the glove as a target for the pitcher.

For maximum stretch, use the fancy title, **Rule of Opposites,** which simply means right hand extended, left foot on the bag, left hand extended, right foot on the bag. The distance between safe and out on most plays is only a matter of inches. Not stretching far enough, not

TIP LEVEL	INFIELDING

using the corners of the bag, not using the proper foot often make the difference. For the other guys.

Sometimes 1st basemen take throws from the catcher, usually on bunts or passed balls. Teach your kids to use the **Inside/Outside** Rule to help catchers make those throws. When the throw's coming from fair territory, or from the 3rd base side of foul territory, the 1st baseman sets up alongside the bag in **fair territory and with both arms up,** calling out **"Inside"** to the catcher, letting him know to throw the ball to that side.

When the throw's coming from foul territory on the 1st base side of home plate, set up alongside the bag in **foul territory,** calling **"Outside".** What you don't want is a throw that cuts across the runner's path. Dangerous for both runner and 1st baseman, and guaranteed to lead to an undeserved throwing error on the catcher.

For the 2nd baseman, footwork on the double play pivot is a two-step, **"Left-Right"** sequence. Teach your kids to take the throw with the **left foot on the bag,** plant with the right, turn and throw. Most of the time the 2nd baseman steps **toward the shortstop,** but the step also can be taken backwards. Varying the move makes it more difficult for the runner to break up the double play.

When the 2nd baseman starts the double play, a good way to get rid of the ball quicker is to do a Drop Step just before the ball arrives. This means moving the right foot back a bit, squaring the body toward 2nd base as the shortstop approaches. Doing the Drop Step correctly means not stepping before the throw. Careful, though, this move is pretty advanced and should be tried during a game only after lots of work in practice.

(continued)

TIP LEVEL	INFIELDING

 Teach your shortstops to use a **Glide Step,** also known as a **Brush Step,** when taking the throw on the double play. The left foot is planted on the center field side of the bag, the **right foot** glides or brushes over the bag as he takes the throw, landing on the 2nd base side. The shortstop then plants with the left foot, turns and throws. This **"Left-Right-Left"** sequence allows the shortstop to make the throw to 1st well out of harm's way from the runner.

 When the shortstop **starts the double play,** a version of the Drop Step can be used here, too, by placing the left foot back as the ball approaches, thereby opening up the body toward 2nd base, in much the same way as we just talked about with 2nd basemen. The same warning applies here, too, since it is pretty advanced. But with enough practice, can be a really great way to teach kids to turn the double play just like major leaguers.

 Infielders should learn to take the throw with **both hands up** on the double play. Having both hands up reduces the margin of error on the catch and quickens the release on the throw.

 Don't let your kids camp out on the bag, whether it's on the double play or on a throw from the catcher. Teach them to use the bag as a barrier between them and the runner, **straddling it from the back side** until the throw arrives.

 When tagging runners out, teach your kids to put the glove down on the edge of the bag and wait for the runner to arrive. **Don't reach** - let him tag himself out.

TIP LEVEL | INFIELDING

FASTFACT: Seven of every ten balls are hit to the 3rd baseman's left. Only one in ten is hit to his right. This explains why left-handers should never be asked to play 3rd base, no matter how strong the arm. They have their glove on the right hand, toward the foul line, where ground balls almost never go.

3rd basemen need to be blessed with two things in life in order to prosper: **a good arm and great reflexes.** Make sure your 3rd basemen have **both hands up before each pitch.** Because most batters are right-handed, balls hit directly at a 3rd baseman are usually screamers.

Teach your pitchers **never to throw from the mound** when making the play at 1st base. Throwing from the mound means throwing either uphill or downhill. Have them take a couple of steps to the level grass and then make the throw. There's little risk involved, because on a ground ball back to the mound the batter's only a couple of steps out of the box. And on a bad throw, he winds up at 2nd base.

This also gives the 1st baseman, who's accustomed to playing several steps off the bag, time enough to find the bag, set up, and take the throw. The same applies for 2nd basemen fielding a ground ball, taking a couple of steps toward 1st to ensure a good throw.

Once your infielders get past the basics, it's time to introduce them to the mystifying world of the "Cut-Off" play. If the throw comes from the right fielder toward 3rd base, it's the 2nd baseman to acts the as the Cut-Off man. When the throw comes home, it's the 1st baseman.

(continued)

TIP LEVEL	INFIELDING/OUTFIELDING

When the throw comes from the center fielder toward 3rd base, it's the shortstop who's the Cut-Off man. When the center fielder throws home, it's the 1st baseman. On these throws, it's very important that the 1st baseman is either in **front of the mound** (between the mound and the center fielder) or **off to the side.** Behind the mound (between the mound and home plate) only encourages a bad hop if the throw hits the mound. Being on the mound also makes it much more difficult to turn and make an accurate throw home.

When the throw is from the left fielder to 3rd base, it's the shortstop who's the Cut-Off man. When the throw comes home, it's the 3rd baseman who takes it, with the shortstop moving around to cover 3rd base.

It also might be a good idea to teach your kids the "Double Cut-Off", when the ball is hit in the gap between the outfielders and/or if you're playing on a field where the fences are pretty deep or nonexistent. On this play, the 2nd baseman comes in behind the shortstop if the throw is coming from either the left or center fielder. The shortstop backs up the 2nd baseman if the throw comes from either the center or right fielder. Teach the back-up man to keep a reasonable distance behind the initial cut-off man, in case the throw gets by.

On the Double Cut-Off play involving a throw to 3rd, teach your **1st baseman** to follow the runner toward 2nd base. Sometimes you can catch an unwary runner who's rounded 2nd base by having the 1st baseman there to take the throw back to the bag.

No matter which base the throw is going to, it's the player on the bag who directs the Cut-Off man, yelling out which way to move - left, right, up or back - to make sure that player is perfectly aligned.

| TIP LEVEL | NOW LET'S TALK ABOUT OUTFIELDING |

In a perfect world, every fly ball would fall to earth, softly, gently, and right where your kids happen to be standing at the time. In the real world, the guiding principle to teach your kids about catching fly balls is **Beat the Ball to the Spot.** The one skill that sets great outfielders apart from the rest is the ability to **be there,** in good position to catch the ball and throw it back, **before it arrives.**

The principle of the **Triangle** is just as important to the outfielder as it is to the infielder, with a couple of minor variations. Teach your kids to catch every fly ball between the shoulders and with the hands out front. But not too far. Don't let your kids catch the fly ball with their arms fully extended. This creates a blind spot that can make the ball disappear just before it enters the glove. It doesn't allow them to use the elbows as shock absorbers, either. Tell them to keep the glove **just a bit lower** than the imaginary line between the ball and their eyes.

If your kids are a little more experienced at catching fly balls, you can advance their education by teaching them to **catch the ball on the throwing side,** instead of directly between the shoulders, but only with runners on base who might be tagging up and less than two outs.

Also teach them to **set up a half-step behind** where the ball's going to land, then move forward to catch it. This gives them momentum to make a stronger throw back to the infield. The half-step they take forward should be on the **same side they throw on.**

There's a version of the "Right/Left" sequence that we just talked about regarding infielders that works for outfielders, too. Teach your kids to do a quick "Right/Left" as the ball approaches, only taking those steps toward the ball, instead of laterally, as with the infielders.

(continued)

TIP LEVEL	OUTFIELDING

 There's one more piece of footwork you can add to the mix, called the **Drop Step.** This is a phrase that might be familiar to basketball fans. The Drop Step is the best way to teach an outfielder to go back on the ball. It's not a Crossover, not a Shuffle, just a **diagonal step back** that does two things at once: **(1)** Turns the body immediately to the side the fly ball is on, and, **(2)** buys the player more ground, more quickly, so he can chase it down.

 The **Drop Step** begins with a **90-degree** turn to the side the ball is on. If your kids have difficulty in mastering the Drop Step, tell them to concentrate not so much on the footwork, but on **turning the shoulder first,** based on the irrefutable logic that where the shoulders go, the legs are sure to follow.

DRILL Remembering the drill where you stand in front of your infielders and signal with your arms for either a Crossover or a Shuffle Step, now you can add one more step for outfielders by signaling with an arm extended upward to signal a Drop Step to either side. Combining these six signals into one exercise makes for a terrific way to teach kids proper footwork for playing the outfield.

DRILL You can take this drill one step farther by using a three-part command, telling your kids to "Drop Step", then after a few steps to "Square Up", and then "Throw", working all the elements of chasing, catching and throwing into one motion. Let them pantomime the drill a few times, then use baseballs placed in the glove, transferring them to the bare hand for the throw.

TIP LEVEL	INFIELDING/OUTFIELDING

A real good tip you can give your more advanced outfielders is to let them know that a ball hit toward the line will drift toward the line. What this means, for example, is that a fly ball down the left field line by a right hand hitter will keep drifting toward the line. Conversely, a fly ball down the right field line by the same hitter will drift toward that line. Same for left hand hitters. The reason being that when a hitter pulls the ball, the ball will hook. When he hits to the opposite field, that ball will slice.

Teach your kids to always look for the cut-off man. In fact, to know where he will be, **before** the play develops. That's why you have outfield practice before the game. A **low throw,** even if it gets to the cut-off man on one hop, is better than a high throw that dribbles all the way through the infield. Make the other guys earn every base they get. Missing the cut-off man is a sure way to turn singles into doubles and runners into runs scored.

Finally, let your kids know that to be either a great infielder or a great outfielder they don't need to possess either a strong arm or fast legs. They just need to anticipate where the ball's going to be and try the best they can to get there first, using the things you've taught them.

There are some other things for infielders and outfielders, including what qualifications each kid brings to the position, and you'll find them in the Chapter on **Coaching/Setting the Line-Up.**

AND REMEMBER, IT'S ONLY A GAME...

Chapter 3

Catching

There might be tougher jobs than being a catcher. Rodeo cowboy comes to mind. Maybe window washer at the Empire State Building. But not in baseball. Catching involves a combination of physical and mental talents demanded nowhere else on the field of play. In youth baseball, it seems to be the appointed position for the oversized, under skilled kid. Nothing should be further from the truth. The prototype catcher is strong, durable, compact. Fearless doesn't hurt, either. Look for a kid who really understands the game and loves playing it. Loves it a lot. Because that love will be severely put to the test, every time he gets behind the plate.

Having said all that, and assuming neither you nor your kids have been scared off by now, here's how the position should be played...

The "Baseball Tips" System™:

⚾	Age 10 & Under/Beginner
⚾⚾	Age 12 & Under/Intermediate
⚾⚾⚾	Age 16 & Under/Advanced
DRILLS	Are called out

TIP LEVEL	CATCHING
⚾	Balance is a **catcher's best friend.** To make it your catcher's best friend be sure that the **feet** are **turned slightly outward** and the **heels** are **elevated.** The **upper legs** are **not quite parallel to the ground.** With bigger kids especially, having the upper legs completely parallel can make a catcher set up too high.

(continued)

73

TIP LEVEL	CATCHING

The chest is **tilted forward and the elbows** are **resting outside the knees.** Remember, elbows are a young player's shock absorbers, so keeping them in tight against the body makes a hard job even harder.

Teaching kids to keep their **bare hand behind their back** is a good idea for those just starting out. Many beginner leagues have restrictions on base running, so there's not much jeopardy in teaching younger kids to catch the ball one-handed for now. More advanced kids can be taught to keep the bare hand tucked behind the glove. In either case, tell them to **make a fist** with the bare hand. Foul balls have a way of finding fingertips.

Teach your kids not to reach for the ball, but to let it come to them. Pitchers and umpires prefer "quiet" catchers, the ones who play the position with a minimum of shifting and movement. This also **saves energy,** something any catcher learns to appreciate, long about the fifth or sixth inning of the game.

For a variety of reasons, a good catcher can be a pitcher's best friend. One of the ways a catcher can earn his pitcher some extra strikes is by **learning how to "Frame" a pitch.** Framing means turning the outer edge of the catcher's glove inward, toward the center of the plate, as he catches the pitch. This often will give the umpire the sense that the pitch caught the corner of the plate, instead of being just outside.

"Framing" also can be done on low pitches simply by **"cupping" the glove,** or turning it upward as the ball approaches. The idea is to catch the pitch with a minimum of movement by either the glove or the body.

TIP LEVEL	CATCHING

LET'S TALK ABOUT EQUIPMENT, BEGINNING WITH...

The cup. Don't let your catcher leave home without it. Shin guards should be long enough to run from knee to instep, coming over the top of the shoe, and tight enough so that they won't turn to the side. Chest protectors come in a variety of shapes and sizes, what's important is that it comes far enough around on both sides to protect the ribs. Which also means it has to be strapped on tightly.

A catcher's mask can be the most uncomfortable thing kids can ever be asked to wear this side of a Sunday suit. It has to be, to do the job it's supposed to. Make sure the mask your catcher wears fits properly and gives full protection all the way around to the back of the head. Also make sure it has a **throat guard** that extends down to the chest and is securely tied on.

Human instinct is to avoid danger. Don't be upset with your kids if they develop the habit of flinching or turning away from pitches. Tell them that the equipment they use only works **when they're facing the ball.** Getting your kids not to flinch may just turn out to be the hardest part of teaching them to be a catcher. Once they're convinced they won't be hurt by the ball, everything else will become that much easier. Safer, too.

DRILL

Set your catchers up in front of you, in full equipment and with both hands behind their back. Toss some tennis balls at them from a few feet away, letting them see for themselves that they won't get hurt as long as they don't turn away. Then try the same thing with baseballs, increasing the distance and the speed with each throw.

Blocking pitches in the dirt doesn't require a whole lot more than just getting the body down as quickly as possible. Teach your kids to drop the **glove between**

(continued)

TIP LEVEL	CATCHING

 their legs, keep their **shoulders squared** and **tilt the chest farther forward.** Make sure they understand the key word here is **"Blocking",** not **"Catching".** At every level of baseball more catchers commit passed balls simply because they reach out and try to catch a ball that's in the dirt, or outside their knees, rather than just hitting the deck and smothering it.

 Tilting the **chest forward** on a ball that's in the dirt is another one of those things that goes against the instinct of turning away from danger. But it's a good way to make sure the ball stays in **front of the catcher.**

 Blocking the plate is a matter of positioning more than anything else. Most youth leagues have a "Slide or Avoid" Rule that pretty much takes away the risk of collisions. Still, it's not a bad idea to let your kids know that so long as they stay **lower than the runner,** they shouldn't get hurt. After all, they're the ones with all that equipment.

 Teach your kids that the best way to block the plate is to step out **in front of it,** anchoring the **left foot** to the top left edge. This also gives the catcher a better chance to take the throw cleanly before the runner arrives. There's no reason to remain behind the plate - once the runner touches it he's already safe. **Anchor the foot, catch the ball** and **collapse.** That's just about all there is to it.

 Don't let your catcher establish position **too far up the baseline** unless he absolutely has to in order to take the throw. Don't give the runner room to run around the tag.

TIP LEVEL | CATCHING

FASTFACT: Here's another Multiple Choice Question: What is the average success rate for major league catchers at throwing out runners? (A) 70%; (B) 50%, or (C) 30%; **Answer:** (C) Major league catchers average less than a 30% success rate at throwing out runners, the best of them around 40%.

Success at throwing out runners is less a matter of a strong arm than it is a **quick release.** Teach your kids that a quick throw is far better than a strong one that takes longer to unload. Don't wind up, don't take off the mask, just bring the ball back behind the ear and fire.

To help your catchers get rid of the ball quicker, teach them their own version of the **Drop Step** with runners on base. The catcher places his right foot about **six inches farther back** than the left. Let your kids decide how far back is comfortable. This slight change opens up the throwing side of the body and helps the catcher get rid of the ball quicker. Also teach your catchers to **set up just a bit higher** when there are runners on base.

When using the Drop Step, the footwork on the throw becomes a step-and-a-half process. The catcher takes a half-step forward with the right foot, a full step with the left and fires. Just as with infielders, it's important catchers begin the act of throwing **while still in the crouch,** instead of standing up first and then throwing. And don't waste time by whipping off the mask first.

It might be best not to confuse younger kids with the Drop Step. Instead, teach them a three-step, **"Left-Right-Left"** sequence that allows them to use the body's momentum when making the throw.

(continued)

TIP LEVEL | CATCHING

FASTFACT: Remember, major leagues scouts look for pitchers to be able to deliver the ball to home plate in 1.6 seconds when working from the stretch. A figure that may seem arbitrary, but it relates to the fact that the average time it takes a good base runner to move from 1st to 2nd is 3.6 seconds. Which leaves catchers all of 2 seconds to catch the ball and deliver it to 2nd base. Tell your kids that's why you spend all that time with them working on footwork and a quick release.

The only time a catcher should get rid of his mask is on a foul pop-up. Teach your kids to hold the mask in the throwing hand, find the ball, and toss the mask in the other direction. Catcher's gloves were not designed for catching pop-ups, so make sure they use **two hands** and don't try to catch the ball with the hands above the eyes.

It's the pitcher's job to tell the catcher where the ball is, just as it's his job to call out an infielder's name on a fly ball in the infield.

Teach your catchers to give the signs on the **inside of the right thigh.** Not in the middle. Not down between the legs. Pointing the **right leg at the first baseman** keeps the other team's first base coach from seeing them. Taking the glove and placing it on the **outside of the left leg,** below the knee, makes sure the 3rd base coach doesn't see them, either. Most of the time the catcher signals "1", "2", "3" with the fingers, but there are variations, such as closed fist, open fist, wiggled fingers, that can be used. Choosing his own signs is a good way to let your catcher take charge of the game.

TIP LEVEL	CATCHING

Giving signs isn't only for the pitcher's benefit, but for the middle infielders', as well. Seeing the signs, knowing whether it's going to be a fastball, curve or change-up, allows them to anticipate where the ball might be hit. The shortstop can even **transmit signs** of his own to the center fielder, helping him get a better break on the ball.

Many coaches tend to feel that their closest bond is with the pitcher. Maybe that's because most coaches' kids get to play that position more often than the other kids (check the fine print on the birth certificate). In fact, the closest bond should be with the catcher, because it's the catcher who **sees every pitch, every play,** of every game, right there before his eyes. It's the catcher who's the coach on the field.

As a result, part of the **catcher's** job is to make sure every player knows the situation: **How many outs there are, where the throw is supposed to go, what everyone should do if the ball comes their way.** All of which goes back to the premise that catching is a job requiring a considerable amount of **both physical and mental skills.**

Finally, tell your kids that being a catcher comes with one guarantee: That when they go to bed at night, they'll be the dirtiest, dustiest, tiredest, most banged up kid on the team. Tell them to wear each bump, bruise and scrape as a badge of honor. Because when they wake up the next morning, it will be with a sense of pride and satisfaction in a job very well done not usually known by any of their teammates. And why not? They've earned it.

AND REMEMBER, IT'S ONLY A GAME...

Chapter 4

Hitting

An imagined conversation, between Abner Doubleday & Son:

"**H**ere's what you do... Take a round object, and then try to hit it with a stick. Only the stick is round, too. And heavy. Something the size of a small oak tree should do nicely... Nope, still too easy.

"Let's say you don't get to hold the ball while you're trying to hit it. Some big guy, who looks at you like you stole something from his grandmother, stands a few feet away and throws it as hard as he can. Hopefully, not at you.

"Got that??? OK, so go out there and make me proud."

No wonder that young players ever since have struggled to hit .300. Let the record show that, as testified to by experts ranging from Ted Williams to Charlie Brown, hitting a baseball is flat out the hardest thing to do in sports. Maybe in the universe.

Here are some things that will help make it easier for your kids...

The "Baseball Tips" System₸M:

	Age 10 & Under/Beginner
	Age 12 & Under/Intermediate
	Age 16 & Under/Advanced
DRILLS	Are called out

(continued)

TIP LEVEL	HITTING

When you take all the theories there are on hitting and toss them all into one giant baseball cap, they come down to one simple phrase: **"See the ball, hit the ball"**.

DRILL

There's a terrific exercise you can participate in with your kids that shows the ultimate value of the "See the ball, hit the ball" wisdom. Have your kids focus on an object in the distance - tree, telephone pole, light standard. Now have them make the **shape of a frame** with their hands held out about 12 inches in front of them. Have them look through that "frame" at the object, with both eyes open. Have them close one eye and look at the object. Have them open that eye and close the other, while still looking at the object. One of those two times, the object will have moved out of the frame. Ask them which time that was.

This simple exercise teaches kids that, just as they were born either right or left-handed, they also were born either right or left-"eyed". One eye is always dominant. The **dominant eye** is the one where the object did not move out of the frame while it was open and the other was closed. For most hitters, the dominant eye is one the same side they throw with - right hand throwing, right eye dominant. Left hand throwing, left eye dominant.

Here's the problem for most kids: Their dominant eye is the one that's farther away from the pitcher while they're standing in the batter's box. Even worse for some kids is that fact that they often will **obscure the vision** in that eye from the pitcher by the angle of the head or the tilt of the batting helmet. Teach your kids that it's very, very important to always be able to see the pitcher - and therefore the pitch - with their dominant eye.

TIP LEVEL	HITTING

DRILL

It may sound silly to some kids, but a surefire way to make sure they are seeing the ball with their dominant eye is to **wink at the pitcher.** Just tell them to close their non-dominant eye and check that they can see the pitcher with their dominant eye unobscured. Chances are, winking won't make the pitcher mad, unless the pitcher happens to be that really cute girl in Math class.

Here's one more fact about seeing the ball, one geared more toward the advanced kids who have to face pitchers who throw breaking balls and off-speed stuff. The non-dominant eye, the one that for most kids is closer to the pitcher, is the one that determines the **rotation of the ball** - fastball, curve, change-up. It's the dominant eye that allows **depth perception** - letting hitters know how soon the ball's going to be there.

All of this really means is that, the next time your young hitters come back to the dugout after a swing-and-a-miss for strike three saying, "I could have sworn I saw that pitch all the way", chances are they really didn't. At least not as well as they thought. Just tell them to make sure they can **see the ball clearly** with their dominant eye the next time at bat and everything will work out fine.

NOW THAT WE'VE TALKED ABOUT SEEING THE BALL, HERE'S HOW YOU HIT IT:

We'll start with the bat, and keep it simple - **the lighter, the better.** And there's an easy way to test just how light it should be. Have your kids take the bat in one hand and try to hold it with the **arm straight out**. If they can do this for a few seconds without the bat wavering at all, it's the right weight. Now let's go on from there.

(continued)

TIP LEVEL	HITTING

 Since baseball began, bats have been designed with a knob on the end to help quicken the swing. Given the choice between choking up with a heavier bat or holding a lighter bat down at the end, have your kids go with the lighter bat every time.

 It's been said there are as many theories on hitting as there are players who can't hit. But among them all there is one common element: That good hitting is the result of getting the **bat through the Zone** as quickly as possible. Otherwise known as **Bat Speed.**

 If Bat Speed is the catalyst to good hitting, teach your kids that there are **three things** that make it happen:

(1) Keeping the weight back for as long as possible, followed by,

(2) A short stride, which leads to,

(3) A quick swing.

 Keeping the **weight back** gives the hitter more time to see the ball, to adjust to its rotation, and to decide whether or not to swing. Hitters who commit to pitches too early, transferring their weight too soon, become prime candidates for off-speed pitches, as well as pitches out of the strike zone.

FASTFACT · Multiple Choice Question: If the recommended stride for a young hitter is between 6 - 10 inches, how long is the stride for a major league hitter? (A) 14 - 16 inches; (B) 10 - 14 inches; or, (C) 6 - 10 inches. **Answer:** (C) 6 - 10 inches. Short strides are key to a hitter's success, whether he's eight years old, or twenty eight.

TIP LEVEL	HITTING

A short stride allows the hitter to transfer the weight as the swing progresses with a minimum of movement by the head and upper body. Hitters who move their head too much will have problems hitting balls up in the strike zone. Hitters who open up the shoulder too soon will have problems hitting balls on the outer half of the plate. Short strides also help teach the short, quick swing you want your kids to learn, since the longer the stride, the longer the swing will be.

DRILL

Stand in front of your kids with your feet together. Now stand with your feet far apart. Ask them whether you're still as tall as you were before. The answer you're looking for is "No". This teaches kids that for every 12 inches of stride, they lose up to an inch in height. Considering that a baseball is only three inches in diameter, even an extra half-inch drop of the head and hands can mean hitting the bottom, instead of the top, of the ball. Hitting pop flies instead of line drives.

Teach your kids to land on the **front half** of the front foot. You can define this even further by teaching them to land on the **inside** of the front half. Landing on the inside helps create a stiff front leg to hit against, increasing bat speed and helping to get the head of the bat out front.

Also make sure they land with the front foot **Closed,** meaning still **parallel to the back foot.** Landing with the front foot **Open** - pointing toward the pitcher - means the hip, shoulder, and head will turn away from the ball. It's natural, given the amount of power being generated by the swing, that the front foot will open up **after contact is made.** But only on **inside pitches,** where the hitter is trying to "Turn" on the ball quickly, should the front foot be open when its lands.

(continued)

TIP LEVEL	HITTING

Landing on the outside of the front foot results in a bent front knee as the body's weight is transferred forward. Something else that causes the hip, shoulder and head to fly open too soon. A bent front knee also takes away much of a hitter's power, because it means the wrists don't turn and the head of the bat never gets out front of the hands at the point of contact.

DRILL

Have your kids take off their front shoe (left shoe for right-hand hitters, right shoe for left-handers) and practice some swings in socks or barefoot. Tell them to feel the weight landing on the ball of the front foot, something that's much harder to do when the shoe is being worn. This is good practice on the field or at home in front of a mirror. Small caveat: Make sure there's no bat in hand when practicing in front of the mirror.

Almost every kid who ever played the game started out by setting up in the batter's box in this sequence:

(1) Digging in with the back foot,

(2) Spreading out with the front, and,

(3) Taking a few practice cuts fierce enough to knock down a barn.

Teach your kids to do the **opposite.**

Start by **establishing front foot position** by aligning it with the bevel of home plate, where the sides begin to angle toward the back. Setting up the front foot there helps make sure that contact with the ball is made out in **front of the plate.** Don't let your kids vary more than a few inches away from that starting point.

TIP LEVEL	HITTING

 Standing **too far forward** in the box gives the pitcher an advantage in throwing fastballs by the hitter and can give him nothing but high pitches to swing at. Remember, the pitcher stands on an elevated mound and releases the ball over his head. As a result, it drops about **an inch for every foot** on the way to the catcher.

 Standing **too far back** gives the pitcher an advantage on off-speed pitches. Curve balls only break the last 10 - 15 feet to home plate. Standing a foot farther back than necessary gives the pitcher an extra **10% worth of movement** on the curve ball. It also makes it harder to hit change-ups.

Only after they've established the front foot do they **dig in with the back.** The weight can be evenly distributed along the back foot, but tell your kids to really dig in with the toes. More on that later.

The 3rd thing is to check for plate coverage, and there's an easy way to teach that. Have your kids **extend their arms** out over the plate, and then just **drop the bat.** If they're the right distance away it should cover the whole width of the plate with a couple of inches to spare. Let your kids do this enough times in batting practice so that they'll automatically know where to stand during the games. Drawing lines in the dirt helps them remember.

(continued)

TIP LEVEL | **HITTING**

BAD PICKUP / BAD GRIP

GOOD PICKUP / GOOD GRIP

There's a real simple phrase you can teach your kids to help them remember the proper grip: **"Eight Middle Knuckles, All in a Row".** From the day they first pick up a bat, most kids place the bat in the **palm of the hand,** then **wrap the fingers around** it. What results is a "Middle-Knuckles-to-Big-Knuckles" grip, one that has a tendency to "strangle" the bat and slow the swing. Teach your kids to **cradle the bat** in their fingers, and then **gently wrap the hands** around it. What you'll get is a grip with the middle knuckles lined up. A grip that helps increase bat speed by enabling the wrists to turn at the most critical part of the swing.

TIP LEVEL	HITTING

Another way to teach kids the proper grip is by having them hold the bat upright against their chest, with their elbows parallel to the ground. See how the grip is naturally "Big-Knuckles-to-Big-Knuckles". Now have them push the bat forward, all the way, until their arms are completely extended in front of them. See how the grip has changed, to "Middle-Knuckles-to-Middle-Knuckles".

DRILL

Have your kids swing with the Middle-Knuckles-to-Big-Knuckles grip, then with the middle knuckles lined up. Tell them to listen to the sound the bat now makes as it whistles through the air that much faster. There is no clearer way for a young player to understand the principle of **Bat Speed.**

Some kids will have a hard time remembering the new grip, others an even harder time getting used to it. Explain to them that this is the way the bat **should be held,** and once they feel comfortable with it, they'll never go back to the old way again. To help those having a hard time remembering the proper grip, tell them to make a fist with each hand and stand in front of you, arms outstretched, and hands together. What **you'll be able to see** is how the middle knuckles are **perfectly lined up.** Use a non-toxic, washable marking pen to connect the knuckles and have them check to see the line is straight each time they come to bat.

NOW TO THE REST OF THE STANCE:

The feet are parallel in the batter's box, shoulder-width or just a bit farther apart. Don't let your kids use too wide a stance, that takes the lower body out of the swing. Teach kids just starting out that the feet should be **equi-distant** from home plate, resulting in a stance that's neither **Closed** nor **Open.** More about Closed and Open stances in the Chapter on **Coaching/Game Strategies.**

(continued)

89

TIP LEVEL	HITTING

The classic power hitter's stance is with the front foot, knee, hip and shoulder all turned slightly inward. If you think your kids someday will be big enough and strong enough to drive the ball great distances, there's no reason not to start them off in that direction now. You make the call. Otherwise, just keep it simple and begin with a neutral stance.

The hips serve as the trigger, transferring energy generated by the lower body through the arms and into the hands. Kids who **don't learn** to rotate the hips properly, in effect, become "Arm" hitters, without much power and usually hitting to the opposite field.

DRILL Have your kids put the bat behind their back, cradling it in the crook of the elbows. Now have them rotate the bat back and forth, looking to see how the body weight is naturally transferred from back to front foot as the hips rotate. Also look to see that the back foot comes up at the heel as the weight is transferred forward. This is also a good way to practice keeping the shoulders level on the swing.

A couple of points about bat position: Make sure the hands are directly **over the back foot.** It's OK for bigger kids, those with longer arms, to keep their hands just a bit behind the back foot. But the opposite **isn't true** - don't let your kids, no matter what size they are, carry their hands **inside** the back foot, in other words,

TIP LEVEL	HITTING

between the feet. Some might think this helps kids by shortening the swing. In fact, it does just the **opposite,** since the bat then has to move backward before it can move forward to begin the swing.

Don't let your kids wrap the bat **too far behind the head.** This lengthens the swing and most kids don't have the wrist and arm strength necessary to bring the bat all the way around quickly enough. Teach your kids to have the bat either straight up or angled slightly backward. Don't let them hit with the **bat parallel to the ground** - that takes away too much leverage.

DRILL

To teach your kids the benefit of keeping the bat elevated, have them hold the bat over their back shoulder, but with only one hand. Tell them to close their eyes and think about how heavy the bat feels in a horizontal position. While their eyes are still closed, move the bat to vertical. Ask them whether the bat now feels heavier, the same, or lighter. The answer you'll get is "lighter".

Don't teach your kids to keep the **back elbow all the way up either,** no matter how many times you've seen major leaguers hit this way. Kids aren't as strong as adults and keeping the elbow parallel to the ground makes for a longer swing. Using the analogy of the clock , if the elbow up is 9:00 o'clock, and down is 6:00 o'clock, teach your kids to carry theirs somewhere around 8:00 o'clock. This still gives them the **leverage** they'll need to drive the ball, without making the swing too long.

Just as the back elbow can be kept too high, it also can be kept **too low.** Kids who hit with both elbows pointing down will wind up being ground ball hitters, because they've taken away the leverage needed to drive the ball

(continued)

TIP LEVEL	HITTING

in the air. Smart pitchers will soon learn to pitch them **up in the strike zone.** For some kids, those who can run with the wind, this may not be a bad way to hit, but let that be a decision made several seasons down the road.

Teach your kids to keep the **front elbow** in close to the body, in the shape of a shallow "V". Keeping the front elbow in helps bring the bat through the Hitting Zone quicker. You've probably heard the word "Extension" used when talking about the swing, having the arms fully extended away from the body. This is something to look for on the **Follow-Through.** Kids who begin the swing with both elbows away from the body, something called "casting" by hitting coaches, lose the power to pull the ball and are destined to have slower swings.

Teach your kids to keep their **hands high** before the swing - at the **top of the strike zone** is a pretty good place to start. That way, any ball higher than their hands is not a strike. This also helps them hit down on the ball, resulting in line drives and hard-hit grounders. In other words, **base hits.** Kids who keep their hands too low, down around the waist, have a tendency to upper-cut the ball, lifting the front shoulder on the swing.

Also teach them to keep the **hands still** before the pitch. Movement of the hands, called a "Hitch", causes delays in the swing. This is an on-field application of "For Every Action There's an Equal and Opposite Reaction". Hands that **move up,** have to **move down** before the swing. Hands that move **forward,** have to move **back.** In the language of baseball, keeping the hands still before the swing is called having "Quiet Hands".

Swinging without a hitch might prove to be the most difficult thing you can teach your kids, this side of throwing strikes consistently. For some kids, a hitch

TIP LEVEL	HITTING

might be nothing more than a nervous reaction - a "trigger" if you will - the mind's way of signaling the body it's time to go to work. If you just can't stop your kids from hitching before the swing, let them use one that **moves the hands backward** a little, not up or down.

Sometimes even the best hitter's going to be fooled by the pitch. **Keeping the hands back** preserves enough leverage to hit the ball hard, even if the weight has already moved forward. Move the hands forward with the rest of the body and there's **nothing left** to hit with.

Having **the chin tucked in close to the front shoulder** is a good way to help kids remember to keep the head from pulling out. For some kids it might even be a good idea to tap their shoulder with the chin before the pitch. Let your kids find their own comfort level, but remind them of the benefits involved in what should be just a temporary measure.

Teach your kids that the **most important part of the swing** is those six to ten inches when the wrists turn, the weight transfers, and the head of the bat moves in front of the hands. This also goes back to the earlier point of setting up the front foot **at the bevel** to help ensure that contact is made out in front of home plate.

The **top hand** on the bat is the one that supplies the power, because it's the one that moves the head of the bat in front of the hands. The **palm of the top hand** should be **facing up** at the moment of impact with the ball. The wrists roll over, but only after contact.

You can teach more advanced kids to **"Keep the Hands Inside the Ball"** when trying to pull a pitch on the inner half of the plate. This word picture, imagining the hands running through the Hitting Zone **between the ball and**

 (continued)

TIP LEVEL	HITTING

 the body, is a good way to teach kids to get the hands working as quickly as possible on inside pitches. Which is just one more way of describing Bat Speed.

 If you were to trace the movement the hands make as the swing progresses, it would be in the **shape of a " $\heartsuit$ ",** tilted backward. Where the hands are at the beginning of the swing is the top of the "D". Since the shortest distance between two points is a straight line, the hands move down the "D" to get to the hitting zone as quickly as possible. As the hands work their way through the swing, finishing up with the follow-through, they follow the rounded side of the "D" all the way around to the top.

 Teaching kids the "D" shape on the swing is also a good way to teach them not to flatten the hands at the top of the swing, on the follow-through. **Flattening the swing** at the very end, in essence wrapping the hands around the head instead of continuing upward, shortens the follow-through and takes away some of the power that's been generated.

DRILL | Sometimes, no matter how much teaching your young hitters absorb, they'll still have difficulty hitting the ball consistently. A pop fly one at bat, a weak grounder the next. To help kids learn where the inconsistency comes from, try taping the sweet spot of the bat (six to seven inches with metal, one to two inches with wood) with adhesive tape. The tape should be new (clean). For this drill to work effectively, it's important that the bat is held the same way each swing. Label up, label down. Doesn't matter. After five or six swings, check the tape to see where the points of impact are. Because of the way to top hand rolls under as the swing progresses, the point of impact for some kids may not always be to the side, but slightly under, at roughly 8 o'clock for right handed hitters and 4 o'clock for left handed hitters.

TIP LEVEL	HITTING
DRILL	As practice continues, have your kids check every few swings, looking for consistent points of impact along the sweet spot. The fewer the marks (hitting the same spot, over and over), the better.

Teach your kids not to pull the outside pitch, but to use an **Inside-Out** swing instead. This is where the hands come through the Hitting Zone **before the head of the bat.** A good way to do this is by **relaxing the top hand,** since it's the one that brings the head of the bat forward. Inside-Out swings are a simple way for kids to hit outside pitches because they're mostly a matter of upper body work - more hands and arms, less hips and legs. Once they figure out **how** to do it and **when** to do it, just punching the ball to the opposite field will result in some of the easiest base hits your kids will ever get.

Going the opposite way also is a good way to move the runner along. Let your kids know that **not every good at bat results in a base hit.** A good at bat is when they've made the pitcher throw more than one good pitch to get an out and done something good for the team in the process.

Teach your kids the value of **Directional Hitting,** trying to hit every ball **back where it came from** - whether inside, over the middle, or on the outside of the plate. Directional hitting is one more thing made easier by a short stride. It's also a baseball version of mind and body working together.

The bigger and stronger your kids are, the more you can emphasize **High Hands on the Follow Through.** For younger kids, just tell them that full extension and a complete Follow-Through are things that good hitters strive for and worry about hand position later.

(continued)

TIP LEVEL	HITTING

There's an easy way to tell if your kids have **transferred the weight properly** at the end of the swing. If done right, the front foot will be down and the back foot will be up at the heel. If the front foot is up and the back foot is down, it's a sure sign the hitter didn't get around on the pitch.

Hitters learn what kind of pitches they like to hit best. For **right-handed hitters,** it's usually something **up in the strike zone.** For **left-handers, something down.** This area becomes their **"Zone".** Teach kids to look for a pitch in their Zone early, or when they're ahead, in the count. **Waiting for a pitch in the Zone** is the sign of a patient hitter. Patience is the sign of a good hitter.

Hitting in the Zone is another way of saying **"Don't swing at what the pitcher wants you to swing at, swing at the pitch you want to hit".** This will be especially true in certain situations. A two ball, no strike count is one of those situations. Being the first batter in the inning is another. When it's late in the game and your team is behind is a third.

Waiting for a pitch in the Zone is **not** the same as waiting for a walk. Teach your kids to be aggressive in their Zone, to reward themselves for their patience by really going after a pitch they've been waiting for. Hitting in the Zone is **aggressive,** not passive, baseball. It's smart baseball, too.

FASTFACT: Major league hitters average almost .300 hitting when they're ahead in the count, about .200 when they're behind. Tell your kids this translates into one more base hit in every ten at bats they can have, just by being patient. The best average by major leaguers comes from swinging at the 1st pitch, but for this to work for kids, it presumes a very good sense of the strike zone.

TIP LEVEL	HITTING
DRILL	If your kids are having a hard time learning where their Hitting Zone - or the entire Strike Zone - is, have them take batting practice without a bat in their hands. Taking the swing out of the process is a good way to help them concentrate on pitch location.
DRILL	There's a good way to show your kids where balls are actually hit in relationship to home plate, depending on whether they're inside, over the middle, or outside. Take three **baseballs** and place one at the **outer edge** of home plate. Take the second and place it **12 inches in front of the inside edge.** Take the third and place it on a direct line between the two, about **six inches from the center.** What you're showing them is that pulling the ball means having to be that much quicker with the swing, while going the opposite way on an outside pitch is something they can take more time to do. Pitches down the middle of the plate should be hit right back where they came from.
	This also is a good way to illustrate what happens when a hitter tries to **pull an outside pitch.** With everything in motion that much sooner toward the inside, there's nothing left to hit with if the ball is **outside.**
	Teach your kids not to try and pull **curve balls and change-ups,** but to hit them right **back up the middle.** It's very important that the front half of the body doesn't open up too soon on off-speed pitches. Tell them that if they keep their hands back and the front side "Closed" long enough, chances are they will **pull the ball anyway,** since these are by definition **slower pitches.**
	The difference between different kinds of pitches isn't just speed, it's rotation, too. Teach your kids to look for the rotation of the ball to tell whether it's a fastball, curve

(continued)

TIP LEVEL	BUNTING

or change-up, the moment it leaves the pitcher's hand. Another tip-off is whether the fingers are **behind the ball** at the point of release (fastball) or **off to the side** (curve ball). Or whether the motion has been varied by a **slower delivery** or the drop of an arm (change-up). Almost every pitcher who ever lived gave something away. The more your kids can learn to look for those tip-offs, the more successful hitters they'll be.

Let your kids know that the time to think of all the things you've taught them about hitting, is not when they're in the batter's box. You cannot think and hit at the same time. Tell them to go through their own personal "Checklist" while in the on-deck circle, which includes taking a moment to think about the situation they'll be facing - **how many runners** are on base, **how many outs** in the inning, **what kind of pitch** to look for - **before** they're in the batter's box.

Maybe the best advice of all is to be patient, to wait for their pitch, and to **never** let themselves get discouraged. After all, even the best hitters fail 70% of the time.

AND REMEMBER, IT'S ONLY A GAME...

Chapter 5

Bunting/Base Running

Bunting and base running are part of what's called "Little Ball"-
baseball played one hit, one base, one run at a time. Little Ball is a
great way for young players to learn the rhythms of the game
because it gets everyone involved. Much more fun, too, than just
sitting back waiting for the big kid on the team to hit the home
run. And since, at its heart, baseball really is a game of situations
- small moments that present themselves from the very first inning
to the very last - how well your kids learn to play Little Ball will more
often than not define the difference between winning and losing.

Here's how you can make it work for your kids...

The "Baseball Tips" System™:

⚾ Age 10 & Under/Beginner

⚾⚾ Age 12 & Under/Intermediate

⚾⚾⚾ Age 16 & Under/Advanced

DRILLS Are called out

TIP LEVEL	BUNTING
⚾⚾	We'll start with the #1 Rule of Bunting: Only Bunt Strikes. Makes perfect sense when you stop to think that the object of a bunt is either to move the runner on to the next base, or to allow the batter to get on base himself. Both of which also are served by a base on balls.
⚾⚾	There are two ways to set up for the bunt - one better than the other for kids just starting out. Beginning with

(continued)

TIP LEVEL	BUNTING

 the **Pivot** style, where the batter simply rotates forward on the balls of the feet, leaving the body and the bat at an angle to the pitcher. The advantage of the Pivot is that it's easy to teach and takes less time in the batter's box. It's the style to use when bunting for a base hit. But most of the time, your kids will be bunting to sacrifice, and it's here that the Pivot carries some distinct disadvantages. Which brings us to the old-fashioned way of setting up, something as easy to learn as....

"1,2,3"... And it's taught this way: Call the position the **back foot** occupies in the batter's box, #1. The **front foot** position is **#2.** Now mark a spot that's about a shoulder's width of distance **directly behind** #2, and call it **#3.** Teach your kids to square around for the bunt in this sequence: #2 moves to #3, and #1 moves to #2. See how this turns the batter 90 degrees, setting him up at the front of home plate, squared up, facing the pitcher.

DRILL | Here's a good way to show your kids the advantage of the "1,2,3," style. Have them establish normal position in the batter's box, then rotate forward on the balls of the feet, using the Pivot style. Now tell them to drop the bat over home plate. See how as little as two-thirds of the plate is covered by the bat. Now have them do it "1,2,3," style and drop the bat. See how the entire plate is covered (Illustrated above).

TIP LEVEL	BUNTING

Another advantage is that, since the batter is now set up in the front of the batter's box, the bat is **even with the front of home plate.** This allows the first bounce to be in the soft dirt in front of home plate rather than a kangaroo-bounce off the plate that gets to the fielder that much quicker. Keeping the bat even with the front of home plate also gives the batter more flexibility in bunting to either side of the field.

No matter which style they use, teach your kids to set up with the bat **at the top** of the strike zone. This does two things:

(1) Tells them that a pitch higher than the bat is **not a strike,** and,

(2) Helps make sure they bunt the **top half of the ball.** Make sure they know to bring the bat back on pitches out of the strike zone. Leaving the bat out there will cost them a strike.

Teach them to keep the head of the bat **higher than the hands** when bunting. Bunts are meant to be hit on the ground, not in the air, and keeping the head of the bat up helps ensure that the ball will be hit downward.

If the pitch is low in the strike zone, tell them to **bend even more at the knees** to reach it instead of dropping the head of the bat. Lowering the head of the bat means the bunt will be popped up and bunts that are popped up have a nasty habit of turning into double plays.

Also make sure the elbows are flexed and kept outside the body. Remember, they're the shock absorbers. The top hand is slid about 18 inches up the bat, pinching the bat from behind with thumb and first two fingers. Don't let your kids **wrap the top hand** around the bat - that's a set of bruised knuckles just waiting to happen.

(continued)

TIP LEVEL	BUNTING

 Teach your kids to pretend that the strike zone is several **inches lower** than normal on a bunting situation. For example, the easiest pitch to bunt is a low curve ball. Smart pitchers will try to keep the ball up in the strike zone. Tell them to be patient and wait for a pitch they can handle, one that's down in the strike zone.

 You don't want much forward motion with the bat when bunting. The easiest way to teach your kids how to soften the impact is to tell them to try and **"catch" the ball** with the top hand. This helps instill the idea of bringing the bat back just a bit to cushion the blow, much the same as when they catch a ball in the glove. This might take a while for some kids to master, since for most of them the top hand on the bat is the throwing - not the catching - hand.

DRILL There's a simple two-man drill that helps teach kids the idea of "catching" the ball with the top hand. Just have one kid soft-toss the ball to the other, who's in the bunting position, but with no bat in hand. All the bunter has to do is practice catching the ball with the top hand, retracting the hand just a bit to cushion the impact. This teaches exactly the kind of motion you want on a bunt. Have them do this for a while, then have the bunter pick up the bat and try it for real, letting that "muscle memory" take over.

 The bottom hand on the bat stays down at the knob, acting as a lever to direct the bunt down either the 1st or 3rd base line.

 If the situation calls for moving the runner from 1st to 2nd, the bunt should go along the **1st base line.** Even if your kids play in a league where there are no lead offs,

TIP LEVEL	BUNTING

leaving the 1st baseman free to charge the plate, it's better to have him field the bunt because a righthander will have to turn against his body to make the throw.

When advancing the runner from 2nd to 3rd, tell your kids to bunt the ball along the **3rd base line.** This puts the 3rd baseman in an either/or situation. If he gives up the bag to field the bunt, the runner advances. If he holds the bag and the bunt is dropped in front of him, chances are everybody's going to be safe.

DRILL

No matter the situation, what you don't want is to bunt the ball back to the pitcher. He's closer to the play and his fielding the bunt allows the other players to hold their position. Here's a great way to teach kids this important point. Take three bats, placing one of them about ten feet in front of the mound and parallel to it. Place the other two about 15 feet closer to the foul lines, one pointing toward shortstop, the other toward the 2nd baseman. What you've created is the shape of a triangle. Tell your kids this is the **"Bermuda Triangle":** The place where bad bunts disappear into the pitcher's hands. Teach them to always bunt the ball outside the Triangle, along either the 1st or 3rd base lines.

For kids who are looking to bunt for a base hit, teach them to use the "pivot" style, because it allows the batter a head start out of the box. Remember, though, contact with the ball has to be made while still in **the batter's box.**

(continued)

TIP LEVEL	BUNTING/BASE RUNNING

 Two things to remember **after the bunt's been made:** If a batter makes contact with the ball in fair territory, outside of the batter's box, he's automatically out. And, most advance leagues play with a "Cut-Out" line that runs parallel to the 1st base line, starting half-way up. For plays out in front of home plate, such as a bunt, it's important kids be told they have to run in the lane formed by the base line and the Cut-Out line, or risk being called out for interference.

 Now on to base running, beginning with it's very **own #1 Rule" -** Never make the **first out** of an inning at 3rd or at home, or the **third out** at 3rd. Here's why:

 A runner on 2nd base (in scoring position) with nobody out in the inning is a resource too precious to risk being thrown out at 3rd. There's any number of ways he can score later on, many without benefit of a base hit. As a result, teach your kids to hold on a ground ball in front of them (to shortstop or 3rd base). On the other hand, it's OK to break on a ground ball behind them (1st or 2nd). Don't break on a **ball back to the pitcher** and **make sure the line drive goes through.**

 Success on the base paths is as much a matter of good eyes a fast feet. Teach your kids to run the bases with their heads up and to always look to the coach when the ball's out of view.

 The same principle applies to fly balls: Go halfway on the short fly ball to left, tag up on one hit to right. **Stealing** should be discouraged, too, because heaven help the child - and the coach who sent him - who's **thrown out at 3rd** with nobody out in the inning.

A corollary of Rule #1 would be: Never lead off a base unless you're **absolutely sure** you know where the ball is. Once they get to 3rd base with one out, teach your kids to **automatically tag** on a fly ball, looking to the base coach

TIP LEVEL	BASE RUNNING

to see when to break. Tagging up should be the **first instinct,** because it's easy enough to score from 3rd on a ball that falls in safely, but almost impossible to tag up and then score after the ball's been caught.

The Cut-Out line teaches kids to run in foul territory going from home to 1st on plays around home plate. Teach them to do **just the opposite,** running in fair territory, when going from 3rd to home. There is no Cut-Out along the 3rd base line, and as long as the runner stays **within the base line,** he won't be called out if the throw hits him while trying to score. **Lead off in foul territory,** so they won't be out if hit by a batted ball, but **score in fair, especially on a throw home.**

There's a number of ways you can teach more advanced base runners how to take extra advantage when tagging up on fly balls to the outfield. For example, if they note the outfielder is going **away from the base** they're going toward. Another way is by seeing whether the outfielder is catching the ball on his **throwing or fielding side.** Or, if he's having to turn and throw across his body vs. catching and throwing the ball in one fluid motion.

Some tips for base runners when there are **two outs:**

(1) Go **on the pitch,** when there's a 3-ball, 2-strike count and there is a force play.

(2) Go **on the swing,** when it's a 2-strike count, and there is a **force play.**

(3) Go **on contact,** unless it's a sharply hit ground ball in front of you and there is **no force play.**

When you have a good runner on 1st and a good hitter at the plate with two outs, **try sending the runner.** If he's safe, he can score on a base hit. If he's out, you still have your good hitter leading off the next inning.

(continued)

TIP LEVEL	BASE RUNNING

Sliding is nothing more than perfecting the art of the **two-point landing.** The two points being the outside of the trailing leg (the one that's tucked under) and the butt on that same side. Teach your kids to keep their **hands in front of their body** when sliding, taking away the risk of getting them caught in the dirt. The object is to make contact with the bag as soon as possible, so make sure the **lead leg** is fully extended.

Some kids prefer having batting gloves in their hands when running the bases. This can be a useful tool in reminding them to keep their hands in front of the body when sliding, but the down side for some can be a set of bruised or scraped knuckles after that next slide in the dirt.

More advanced kids can be taught the **Hook Slide,** where the trailing leg "hooks" around the bag in order to avoid the tag, and the **Stand-Up Slide,** on plays when there's the chance of advancing to another base. With the Stand-Up Slide, the runner pushes upward with the trailing foot to help him get upright again more quickly. Not recommended for younger kids, or those who are allowed to play in steal cleats. There's no reason to let a fancy-move-gone-bad take away an entire season.

DRILL It's much easier to teach proper sliding techniques by having your kids take their cleats off and practice sliding in the grass. For more advanced kids, try dropping your glove to one side of the bag or the other just before they slide, teaching them to aim for the other side to avoid the tag.

Though it may look good from the stands, there's no real point to sliding into 1st base. Every inch of the time a runner is traveling through the air, gravity is slowing

| TIP LEVEL | BASE RUNNING |

him down. Teach your kids to run hard all the way through the bag and to touch the nearest edge, instead of on top.

There are three commands the runner and 1st base coach should know:

(1) "Run Through the Bag", for close plays at 1st. Teach your kids to turn toward foul territory after they hit the bag, so they won't run the risk of being tagged out.

(2) "Make the Turn", on balls hit into the outfield where there might be the chance for extra bases. Here, the runner "rounds off" the bag by taking his last steps in a tight, counter-clockwise arc that sends him directly toward 2nd, and keeps running until he's told either to turn back or go on to the 2nd base.

(3) "Take Two", which means go on to 2nd base. Runners also should learn to hit the inside of the bag and to pick up the 3rd base coach for instructions before reaching 2nd base, especially if the ball is hit behind them.

If your kids play in a league where leading off is allowed, teach them **never to use a Crossover Step** while getting off the base. Use a **Shuffle Step** instead, making sure the feet never come together. The Crossover involves a transfer of weight forward, making it more difficult to get back to the bag when there's a throw from the pitcher. There is **no greater sin** in baseball than getting picked off.

Teach these kids to lead off the base in a **direct line** to the next base. The shortest distance between two points is a **straight line,** so leading off on a line between the base saves inches that can make the difference between safe and out.

(continued)

TIP LEVEL	BASE RUNNING

The other benefit of leading off in a direct line is that it cuts down the **visual angle** between the pitcher and the runner, leaving the illusion in the pitcher's mind that the runner isn't as far off the base as he really is.

If your kids play in a league where leading off is **not allowed,** teach them to anchor the **left foot** to the bag. This leaves them free to see the entire infield and, since most kids are right-handed, gives them the advantage of pushing off with the stronger right foot.

Don't let your base runners stand with their hands on their hips or on their knees. Teach them to keep the **elbows flexed** and the **hands out front** for better balance and a quicker break. Use the hands to help "throw" the body toward the next base. Make sure the **knees are flexed,** too, because the lower the center of gravity, the easier it is to get the body moving.

In either case, teach your kids to use the **Crossover Step** when breaking to the next base, because it gains the most ground in the least amount of time and gets the body moving forward more quickly. Also teach them that the first few steps after the Crossover are **short, choppy ones** to help them get to full speed as quickly as possible.

Teach your kids there are differences between Stealing and the Hit-and-Run. On the Hit-and-Run, the runner looks back to see **whether** the ball's been hit and **where.** He shouldn't look back on the Steal. Remember, the Hit-and-Run is not a steal - it's an attempt to let the batter advance the runner - so the runner should be more cautious leading off. No reason to get picked off. Teach the batter to swing at the pitch, no matter where it is, to protect the runner by keeping the catcher from coming forward.

TIP LEVEL	BASE RUNNING

 A similar principle applies to **stealing home.** If the runner breaks too soon from 3rd, it gives the pitcher time to throw a Pitch-Out.

 The Hit-and-Run and the Suicide Squeeze are "Time Specific" plays. Hit-and-Run early in the inning and when the count is in the **batter's favor.** Suicide Squeeze with **one out in the inning.** Another application of the #1 Rule of Base running.

 Most plays in baseball are only a matter of inches. Teach your kids that it's the **first steps out of the batter's box,** and not the last steps into the base, that mean the difference between safe and out, and between singles and doubles. Also teach them to keep the eyes open and the head up on the base paths, and to look **for the ball first,** then **look for the base coach.**

 FastFact: The best base stealers are successful 75% of the time. Being successful only 50% of the time is the mark of a bad base runner.

 Good base running, like good bunting, is more a matter of concentration than skill. The best base runners are not always the fastest, but the ones who survey the entire field around them, know whose arm is strong and whose is weak, and above all else understand that baseball is a game of situations. Speed is the only skill that comes to the ballpark every day so use it well, use it wisely, and use it often. Teaching kids how to use it is something that comes with time, experience, and a little patience. On the part of both player and coach.

AND REMEMBER, IT'S ONLY A GAME...

Chapter 6

Coaching/Setting the Line-Up

Experience suggests a coach's job description is written in two parts: Teach the kids in practice; put them in a position to win during the games. Realizing that not every parent is a Coach (just as not every Coach is a parent), this section of the book, including the Chapters that follow on practice drills, game strategies and trouble-shooting, is for those brave souls who accept the challenge and reward of teaching baseball not just to their kids but to an entire team. Consider it an appeal to self-preservation. Remember, as volunteer coaches we're all working on one-year contracts.

And, having been there, I can bear witness to the fact that is it truly one of life's most embarrassing moments to have a squad of ten-year-olds turn and ask, "What do we do now, Coach?", only to find you sporting that "deer-caught-in-the-headlights" look.

We'll begin with Setting up the Defense...

HERE'S WHAT TO LOOK FOR, IN DECIDING WHO PLAYS WHERE:

PITCHER: | Strong-armed, athletic, able-to-handle pressure, these are obvious prerequisites. But there's one more that outweighs all those combined: Willing to learn. Pitching is such a delicate, precise art that it's almost impossible to teach young throwers how to become pitchers unless they don't also possess the desire - and the patience - to learn how to do it right.
Good students make good pitchers.

CATCHER: **Not the place** to stick the oversized, under skilled kid, despite evidence to the contrary in every kids' baseball movie ever made. In fact, the bigger the player is, the harder it is to be a good catcher. The prototype is **strong, fearless, compact.** It's a position that will test your kids' love for the game, every time they get behind the plate. I've always told kids on my teams that this is the quickest way to the big leagues. What I didn't tell them is that it's the toughest position to play... and there really isn't a close second.

1ST BASE: Natural spot for left-handers and players with weak arms. Also traditionally thought of as a position occupied by good hitters. But lots of successful players have framed their entire careers around the one skill a good first baseman alone has to possess: The ability to dig the ball out of the dirt. Look for a kid with **good hand-eye coordination** and the rest is easy.

2ND BASE: Good middle infielders (shortstops and 2nd basemen) share a number of physical and mental skills in common. The ability to **understand the rhythms** of the game and to anticipate what's going to happen next are very important here. A 2nd baseman tends to be smaller and has a weaker arm than the shortstop, but with the same good hands and quick feet. Think of a ballet dancer in cleats.

SHORTSTOP: If you were using football players on your team, this is where you'd put the quarterback. What you want is a kid blessed with a strong arm and exceptional range. More than that, it's the ability - and the confidence - **to take charge** in the infield that separates the really good shortstops from the rest. Probably the place you'd want to play your best athlete.

3RD BASE: Don't be tempted to put a left-hander here, no matter how strong the arm. **Seven of every ten** balls are hit to a 3rd baseman's left. Only one in ten is hit to his right. A left-hander has the glove on the wrong side to be an effective fielder. Find a kid who can concentrate and has quick reactions. Since most hitters are right handed, a ball hit directly at a 3rd baseman is usually a screamer.

LEFT FIELD: Try a right-handed kid here, because that gives him a natural advantage in throwing to second base. This is a terrific place to reward someone who may not have the skills to play the infield, but who, by learning how to back up throws and hit the cut-off man, can be made to feel he's an important part of the team. Know what? **He is.**

CENTER FIELD: Shortstop of the outfield. This is the only outfielder who has to be equally good at going to his left and to his right. Like the shortstop, he should have a special feel for the game. If your center fielder's disappointed at not being part of the infield, tell him **the best who ever played the game,** played his position.

RIGHT FIELD: Great place for a strong, left-handed kid. His throw to 3rd base is the longest for any outfielder, but it's made easier by being left-handed. Speed is not important here, especially if you have it in your center fielder and 2nd baseman. We'll talk about the batting order momentarily, but chances are your right fielder will also wind up being one of your **power hitters,** as well.

NOW, THE BATTING ORDER:

3RD: Let's simplify things right from the start: Look over your team. Pick out your best hitter. And put him **3rd in the lineup.** This is the one spot where the ability to get on base and drive in runs is paramount. And isn't that another way of describing the best hitter on the team???

LEADOFF: The true measure of a leadoff man's success isn't batting average, but on base percentage, defined as how often your leadoff hitter's able to **get on base** by whatever means. A good OBP can be as much as 100 points higher than a batting average. Look for a kid who knows the strike zone, is a patient hitter and can run holes through the wind. The job of a leadoff hitter is very simple: Get on base.

(continued)

2ND: Might be the **hardest place to be a good hitter** in the entire lineup, because it requires someone who can take some pitches, bunt, hit behind the runner, and in general be willing to take the bat out of his own hands for the good of the team. This is a spot where a low batting average still could indicate a job well done. A job **very well done.**

4TH: Forever referred to as the "Clean-Up" spot - the place where home run hitters reside. Just as On Base Percentage is a better yardstick than batting average for your leadoff hitter, Slugging Percentage (total bases divided by number of official at-bats) is a better way to measure the productivity of your Clean-Up hitter. But, **don't be tempted** to put your best hitter here. Players gifted with great strength usually are not also gifted with great speed. And remember, the farther down the lineup, the less often he'll get to bat.

5TH: Perfect spot for the steady, dependable, line-drive hitter, the kind you want at the plate with runners on base and two outs in the inning. Put your **2nd best pure hitter here.** This is a spot where foot speed is not a high priority, because it will be his bat, not his legs, that manufactures runs for you.

6TH: Not a bad place for the **big swinger,** the kind of kid whose failures are as spectacular as his successes. Operate on the general assumption that every so often, there's going to be a situation where the 6th spot comes up with the chance to really help the team. Then accept whatever happens.

7TH: In the major leagues, this is a spot that tends to be occupied by slow-footed hitters with long swings. But in youth baseball, try to think of it as a **mini-version** of the leadoff spot. You'll be surprised how often the 7th hitter bats first in the inning for you. And if you're in a program where you'll have kids for more than one season, this is a great chance to help a younger player learn the skills of a leadoff hitter, which he'll be able to put to good use the following season.

8TH: See 7th, especially as it applies to younger players. Add earlier comments about 2nd spot. Then sit back and watch him develop, while looking forward to next year.

9TH: This is a good spot to involve, and maybe challenge, a kid whose skills need time to develop and from whom little is expected now. The kind of kid who'll benefit from the absence of pressure. And as a result, anything that happens will be a pleasant, if unexpected, bonus. For you and for him.

AND REMEMBER, IT'S ONLY A GAME...

Chapter 7

Coaching/Practice Drills

Depending on your natural outlook on life, running a baseball practice with a group of kids is a revelatory experience most closely akin to (A): A well-precisioned exercise run with the timing and discipline of the invasion at Normandy, or, (B): A lot like trying to get cats to march in a parade.

It's worth saying again: Baseball is a game of situations - small moments that present themselves, from the very first inning to the very last, that more often than not define the difference between winning and losing. Each of these practice drills is designed to help prepare your kids for those small moments. Even more importantly, they help kids learn to work together, to anticipate each other's movements, and to understand each other's responsibilities. Something called "Teamwork".

Running a practice is all about time: Using it to your and your players' best advantage. The governing principle being that practice time is most effectively spent when everyone is doing something that's both constructive and instructive, every minute they're on the field.

3 KINDS OF PEPPER
Cold, Hot and On One Knee

Anyone who's ever gone to a baseball game knows that "Pepper" games are a regular part of pre-game warm-ups. Pepper also is a great practice tool - it's easy to set up, takes little space and can involve everyone on the team. It's best played in groups of 3 to 6 kids, one hitting, the others fielding. Pepper is about **hand-eye coordination** - hitting the ball with the head of the bat in front of the hands. And just so no one gets bored, it comes in three basic flavors: **Cold, Hot and On One Knee.**

(continued)

COLD PEPPER | is a fancy way of describing Pepper played the old-fashioned way, in which the player who catches the ball throws it back to the hitter.

HOT PEPPER | takes the **fielding part** of the drill one step farther. In Hot Pepper, the player who fields the ball flips it to the player on his right, and so on down the line until it winds up in the hands of the player **at the end of the line.** It's the player on the end of the line who always throws it back to the hitter. This simple variation helps fielders practice hand-eye skills as well, and since one of the rules of Pepper is that a fielder who drops the ball goes back to the wrong end of the line, this helps keep the concentration levels up, too.

ON ONE KNEE | is for the benefit of the **hitter,** especially one who can use extra practice developing bat speed. The hitter gets down on one knee, the **front knee,** and hits the ball. This takes the **lower body** out of the hitting equation entirely, allowing the player to concentrate on hands and upper body. Make sure each one of your players has at least one round of **On One Knee,** in every Pepper game.

Also make sure your kids understand that Pepper is **not** synonymous with Home Run Derby. Tell them to loosen the grip on the bat and back their hands up a few inches, to hit the ball softly enough that it can be fielded easily and painlessly by the other kids involved. Tell them to concentrate on the bat meeting the ball, keeping the head still and looking to see that the head of the bat is out in front of the hands on contact.

To make it more fun, let the **hitter call out** which kind of Pepper he wants to play during his time at bat.

THROWING DRILL
Relay Lines

Kids should be taught always to turn **toward their glove-hand side** when throwing the ball to a player behind them, whether it's the pitcher trying to pick-off a runner at 2nd, or an infielder taking a relay throw.

THROWING DRILL
Relay Lines (cont.)

Have your kids make up two long lines, anywhere from 60 to 120 apart, depending on their size and skill levels, and start the drill by having the player at the beginning of each line throw to the next player in line. Each player stands squared up with both hands up, facing the player throwing to him, then turns to the glove-hand side and throws to the one **behind him.** When the ball get to the player at the end of the line, he throws it back to the player he just got it from, beginning the cycle again. This drill puts a premium on making both good catches and good throws, honoring the baseball axiom that there are two parts to every play. Having two lines allows for some friendly competition among teammates.

After a few cycles, let the players on the ends of the lines trade places with those in the middle. More advanced kids can be taught to "open" the glove-hand shoulder, turning just before the ball arrives.

THROWING DRILL
Throwing the Ball to a Spot

One of the best drills you can use to teach kids that baseball empha-sizes quickness and hand-eye coordination is one that involves throw-ing the ball to a spot, **before** the other player gets there. Use two bases and divide your kids into two groups, each group forming a line alongside a base, six to ten feet from it. What you'll have is two paral-lel lines of kids, facing each other from a base path's distance away.

The first player begins the drill by running to his base, turning and throwing, **not to the other player, but to the other base.** It's only when the ball is in the air

(continued)

that the first player in the other line runs to the base, straddling it to receive the throw, then throws the ball back. The **second player in the first line** then breaks to catch and return the throw. Make sure the player who's just thrown the ball moves out of the way so the next player can have a turn. Keep the drill going, until each player in each group has had a chance to participate.

Once your kids get the hang of this drill you can extend it through several cycles by having each player who's thrown the ball back keep moving to the **other side of the base,** forming a new line to go back the other way again. This is a terrific drill for everyone, but especially **middle infielders,** for working on footwork for the double play, and **catchers,** for learning to throw the ball quickly on an attempted steal.

2 - MAN BASEBALL
Shortstop & 2nd Baseman

In keeping with the idea that practice time is most effective when spent in small groups, shortstops and 2nd basemen can work together practicing their footwork on the double play.

All this drill really needs is two players and one base. Referring to the Section on **Infielding,** for the shortstop it's a three-step, "left-right-left" sequence over the bag, using the **Brush Step** or **Glide Step.** For the 2nd baseman, it's a two-step, "left-right" sequence, touching the bag with the left foot, planting and throwing with the right.

Let each player "Coach" the other by looking to see that he approaches the bag with both hands up, straddles it before the throw, and lands far enough out of the way to avoid the runner. Have them mark spots in the dirt each time to check their footwork. This drill works best when the players begin a small distance from each other, then extend the distance gradually.

Let your kids run through this drill a few times **without a ball,** allowing them to concentrate on footwork, instead. Then add a coach or other player to assume the role of 1st baseman on the throw.

---

3 - MAN BASEBALL
Pitcher, Catcher & 1st Baseman

If the double play is the **prettiest** play in baseball, then the **ugliest** surely must be the ground ball to the right side, where both the pitcher and the 1st baseman go to field the ball and nobody covers the bag.

This drill begins with the pitcher throwing the ball to the catcher, who then rolls the ball to the right side, between the mound and 1st base. Pitchers should be taught to always **break a few steps** toward the bag on any grounder to the right side, anyway, and this drill teaches him to keep moving until the 1st baseman calls the play.

If the 1st baseman - or occasionally the 2nd baseman when the 1st baseman is drawn off too far to get back in time - fields the ball, the pitcher runs to a spot **along the base line** about ten feet from the bag, then runs up the line to take the throw. Teach the 1st baseman to give the pitcher a throw he can handle, **before** he gets to the bag, leaving him time enough to field the ball cleanly and make the play.

Teach the pitcher to take the throw on the **inside,** not the top, of the bag, and get away from it as soon as the out is made. If the 1st baseman indicates he's going to the bag himself, the pitcher moves out of the baseline, away from the runner.

This drill helps your kids understand that on this play it's only the pitcher or the 1st baseman who covers the bag. It's too difficult - and much too **dangerous -** a play for the **2nd baseman,** who is forced to run full speed toward the bag in a collision course with the runner.

For both players, it's a good idea to simulate a situation where there's another runner on the bases, so that whoever makes the out turns quickly to see if the runner's **trying to take an extra base.** Games have been lost during every season, at every level of baseball, just because somebody assumed a play was over before it really was.

The catcher's job is to **run up the line** in foul territory, backing up the throw, just the same as he would be doing on any other play in the infield. Reason #127 why the catcher's job is the toughest in baseball.

---

4 - MAN BASEBALL
Outfielders

Pair off your outfielders and have them stand in two lines, about 15 feet apart. Though the suggestion here is for four kids, this drill can be conducted with **any even number** of players you wish to use. Give each player in one line a baseball and tell him he's got **six options:** Throw a ground ball to either side, throw a fly ball to either side, or throw a fly ball behind the other player, to either side.

This is a footwork drill, so make sure the player(s) throwing the ball look for either **Shuffle** or **Crossover Steps** on the ground balls, Crossovers on the flyballs to either side, and **Drop Steps** on fly balls thrown behind.

You also can involve coaches in this drill by having one stand behind the line of players receiving the throws and signalling to the players throwing the ball which kind of play to work on. Referring to the Chapter on **Outfielding,** the signals can be: **arm down** for grounders to either side, **arm extended** for flyballs to either side, and **arm upright** for flyballs behind to either side.

---

6 - MAN BASEBALL
Bunting Defense Drill

There are two ways to defense bunt plays and this drill allows your kids to work on each. The first, which will be used when there is a **runner on 1st base,** begins by having the catcher roll out a bunt. This is what happens next:

The **pitcher, 1st and 3rd basemen** break to the ball. The **2nd baseman** covers 1st base, and the **shortstop** covers 2nd. It's the catcher's job to call out the play, deciding who picks up the ball and to which base it is thrown. If he doesn't make the throw himself the **catcher's job is to cover 3rd,** preventing the runner from taking an extra base.

The other defense, commonly known as the **Wheel Play** is one put into effect when there's a runner on 2nd and the attempt is to bunt him over to 3rd. On the Wheel Play, the **shortstop** moves to cover 3rd and the **2nd baseman** moves to cover 1st, leaving 2nd base unoccupied. There's an important difference in the **1st baseman's** role here in that, since 1st base is unoccupied or there's a runner on 2nd as well as on 1st in this situation, he's free to leave his normal position more quickly and charge the bunt more aggressively. The **first option** on this play is to have the 1st baseman field the ball and throw to the shortstop covering 3rd. Failing that, the throw goes to the 2nd baseman to get the out at 1st base.

You **can involve the entire team** on this and other kinds of infield drills by teaching the outfielders to back up bases and hit the cut-off man. The cut-off man on throws home from left field is the 3rd baseman. It's the 1st baseman or throws home from center or right. Make sure 2nd and 3rd base are covered by the middle infielders.

You also can **save time** during infield/outfield practice by having **two coaches** hit balls, one standing a few feet up the 3rd base line from home plate who hits to the 1st baseman, 2nd baseman and some outfielders on the right side of the field, while the other stands a few feet up the 1st base line and hits to the shortstop, 3rd baseman and outfielders on the left side.

CATCHER'S DRILL
Blocking Pitches

During times when the rest of the team is otherwise involved - during batting practice, for example - have your catchers work together on blocking pitches in the dirt. All you need is two kids, one set of equipment, a ball, and some dirt. Have one catcher short-hop some balls to the other, who's in full gear, looking to see that he drops the glove **behind the legs,** stays squared up with the shoulders, and points the chest **forward.** Make sure they do this drill **on dirt -** balls bounced on the grass are too easy to block.

(continued)

PITCHER'S DRILL
Long-Tpss/Wind Sprints

When they're not throwing during batting practice, pitchers can work together in a couple of ways: **Throwing long toss** is one that helps extend the arm muscles by throwing from distances farther than the usual pitching distance. In Long-Toss, make sure your pitchers know to push off the back leg and **get some arc** on the ball. This isn't "Burn-Out" - it's an exercise meant to loosen the arm muscles and is a very good use of time for pitchers who aren't otherwise occupied.

Running wind sprints is something else pitchers can do. **Talking among themselves** about certain hitters and certain situations is a third. Practice for pitchers should involve drills that develop **both the physical and mental skills they'll need during the game.**

BATTING PRACTICE
Breaking Hitters Down, Piece-by-Piece

The good thing about batting practice is that it's the best way for hitters to become better. The bad thing is that's it's slow, cumbersome work, involving only a few players at a time. Unless you run it this way:

To help quicken the pace of batting practice have **one player "Shag"** for the pitcher, standing alongside him, feeding him balls and taking throws that come back to the mound. After the hitter has finished, the player Shagging gets to come off the field for his pre-batting practice drills and another player assumes the job of Shagger.

Have **only three players off the field** during batting practice. One at bat, another on-deck, and one "In the Hole", involved in some **pre-batting practice** drills. Like Soft-Toss for hitters:

In Soft-Toss, a coach tosses some balls to the hitter from a safe angle alongside. The object in Soft-Toss is to develop hand speed, so make sure the tosses are over the batter's front foot. Also do it while the batter is down on one knee. Baseballs have a way of tearing up fences, especially when they're hit from short distances away, so use some **tennis balls or rubber balls.** Your neighborhood ground keeper will thank you for it. Hand speed can also be developed by having the coach throw some rubber or plastic balls from a short distance away.

The **player On-Deck** takes the time not just to collect his helmet and bat, but also to collect his thoughts. Mention was made in the **Section on Hitting** that you cannot think and hit at the same time. This goes for batting practice as well as for games. Teach your kids to take this time to think about what they **want to accomplish** during batting practice - weaknesses in their swing to be improved on, or bad habits to be corrected. Then let them come to the plate prepared to work as hard and as long as necessary to get these things done.

Teach your kids to **gradually** work into **hitting the ball hard** in batting practice. Lay down some bunts first. Take a few easy swings before cutting loose. Batting practice, like Pepper, is **not** Home Run Derby. Hitters who use the time to see just how far they can hit the ball in batting practice, usually **will not hit it very far** during the game.

A few words about **batting tees and pitching machines:** These are time-honored devices used by hitters in every level of baseball. But to use them effectively it should be understood what they're designed for and what their limitations are. The batting tee is good for directional hitting - hitting the inside pitch early, using an Inside-Out swing on the ball that's away. Tees also are good for keeping the **shoulders level,** hitting **down on the ball,** and developing the **top hand.**

Hitting in the cage is by nature a repetitive act - the same ball coming at the same height, at the same speed. This makes batting cages a terrific place for **isolating problems,** working on one thing at a time until the problem is solved, and then going on to something else.

Neither the cage nor the tee is a real substitute for live pitching, but both can have important roles to play in the development of young hitters, if used for the right reasons.

125

(continued)

THE RUN-DOWN PLAY
Laurel & Hardy in Pinstripes

No discussion on practice drills would be complete without attention being paid to the Run-Down Play, especially for those who have learned to appreciate physical comedy at its best.

There are only three options on the Run-Down play:

(1) You get the runner out;

(2) The runner's safe at the base he started from;

(3) He's safe at the base he was going to.

Teach your kids to **try for #1,** to **settle for #2,** and **never accept #3.**

Begin with the premise that it shouldn't take a whole roster's worth of kids just to tag one poor guy out. Run-Down Plays are basically **3-man baseball,** involving the player who initiates the throw, and two others who covers the bases. It's really not all that complicated, so long as each player understands that after he throws the ball to a base, his responsibility is to go cover that base. Something called **following the throw.**

The next thing to remember is to **stop the runner's progress early.** This is done by running directly at him or by throwing to the base he's going to, once he's halfway there. The thrower then goes to **cover that base,** since the player he's just thrown it to is now chasing the runner back the other way. That player throws to the 3rd player only when the runner is **10 to 12 feet** from that base, close enough for that player to tag him out.

Teach your kids that the best thing to do in a situation when they've just been thrown the ball on the Run-Down and the runner's already moving to the next base is to get rid of the ball quickly, throwing it to the teammate ahead in an effort to make the runner stop and turn back toward the base from whence he came.

A well-executed Run-Down play is one that takes only one throw after it's begun. Teach your kids **never to chase the runner** toward the next base - the pursuit always should be back to where he started. Even if he arrives there safely, hopefully, he'll be exhausted enough from the effort not to want to leave the base for some time to come. More advanced kids can be taught to **cut down the distance** on the throw. For example, if the play begins with a pick-off at 1st base, the 1st baseman should move toward the pitcher when the ball is on the way, saving time and giving him a better angle to make the throw.

Don't feel bad if your kids can't execute the Run-Down play. There are guys making millions of dollars a year who don't do it very well, either. Just sit back, enjoy it, and hope for the best. And have the video camera handy, just in case something really funny happens.

A final word about how best to develop a young player's skills: It's very trendy to see kids working with weights or on exercise machines in order to improve their skills. Remember, though, baseball is a **reactive, not an active,** game. One that puts a premium on speed and flexibility, not size and strength. Do whatever you think is best for your kids, but it might be a good idea to back off on the weights and just let them swim, run, ride bikes and play basketball. In other words, all those things kids have been doing since toys and games were invented.

Oh, and one more thing. Let them **play baseball,** too. Lots of it.

AND REMEMBER, IT'S ONLY A GAME...

Chapter 8

Coaching/Game Strategies

It's been mentioned here that baseball is a game of small moments. It's also a game of "Ists". More runs are scored in the Ist inning of the game than in any other. The team that scores Ist wins 70% of the time. The team that gets the Ist batter on base in an inning scores 70% of the time. The natural ebb and flow of the game dictates that any coach, at any level, does everything he can to take advantage of those "Ist" opportunities, every time they present themselves.

And that includes game strategies like these...

FIRST PITCH STRIKE
Putting the Numbers on Your Side

There's a truckload of statistical evidence to suggest that the very best thing a pitcher can do is get **ahead in the count.** Batting averages drop almost 100 points when the batter is hitting behind, rather than ahead. Remember, **pitching is the art of making the batter swing at pitches you want him to hit,** not at pitches he wants to hit. Hitting behind in the count forces the hitter to swing at pitches not necessarily in their "Zone", another explanation for that 100-point drop in average.

Teach your kids to throw a **Ist pitch strike** to every hitter, every time. The worst that happens is the batter puts the ball in play. Even then, your pitcher has a 70% chance that his teammates will get him out.

More advanced kids can be taught, however, that not every strike needs to be down the middle. Teach them to work the **Corridors** of home plate: Inner half/outer half, up/down. Even the best hitters have a

(continued)

"Zone" that covers no more than half the plate. Teach your kids to think of the battle between pitcher and hitter this way: Let the batter command one half of the plate, let the pitcher command the other half.

But it's the **pitcher who decides which half of the plate is his.**

FIRST BATTER ON/FIRST BATTER OUT
Putting Pressure on the Other Guys

The job of the leadoff hitter in an inning, whether he bats 1st, 5th, or 9th in the lineup, is very simple: Get on base. It's not a bad idea to have your leadoff hitter take a strike, especially if it's a kid with a long swing and an uncertain sense of the strike zone. Otherwise, preach "Zone" to your leadoff hitters. Preach it again. Then preach it some more.

There's another benefit to having the leadoff hitter take some pitches, especially when it's **early in the game.** Make the pitcher word hard, throwing more than one good pitch to get an out early in the game, and chances are he won't be there at the end.

On the other side of the ball, teach your 3rd basemen - 1st basemen, too - to play shallow on the leadoff hitter. Make the other guys earn the right to get on base. Bunts, intentional or otherwise, will not be accepted. Playing shallow might make your kids vulnerable to a ball hit down the line, but remember that only **one in ten** balls is hit down either line. The rest are hit toward the center of the field, so playing shallow is a pretty risk-free proposition that can pay big dividends for your team.

Playing shallow at the corners is also a way to help protect the pitcher, since early in the inning, early in the game, he's concentrating more on getting his rhythm, throwing strikes, and less on **fielding his position.**

FIRST RUNNER ON/FIRST RUNNER HOME
Turning the Pressure up a Notch

As a coach, get the 1st runner on in the inning and any number of possibilities present themselves for getting him home. You can bunt, steal, Hit-and-Run. All to get the **runner into scoring position** with less than two outs. When you have a runner on 2nd base with one out, try getting him to 3rd by using something called the **"Show Play"**. You always want to bunt down the 3rd base line when trying to get the runner to 3rd. The Show Play is a way to force the 3rd baseman into making decisions that he doesn't necessarily want to make. Here's how it works: Have your batter "Show" the bunt by **squaring around early -** before the pitcher is into his windup or into his stretch. Check the 3rd baseman. If he charges, the batter takes the bat back and the runner steals 3rd. If he holds the bag, bunt the next strike down his way. The 3rd base coach is an important part of this play, using verbal commands to help the batter know what to do.

Get the runner to **3rd base with less than two outs** and there are a number of ways to score without benefit of a base hit. A ground ball to the middle infielders if they're playing back - just make sure the pitcher doesn't field the ball. Tag up on any fly ball. Try the Suicide Squeeze when there's one out in the inning and less than two strikes in the count. Remember, the Suicide is **not a steal of home.**

And above all else, abide by the **#1 Rule of Baserunning:** Never make the 1st out of an inning at 3rd or at home, or the 3rd out of an inning at 3rd.

A good way to make sure the **other team's runners don't advance** without earning the right to do so is to have your shortstop come halfway between the mound and 2nd base on **every throw back** from the catcher to the pitcher.

PICK-OFF PLAYS
Among a Pitcher's Very Best Friends

If your kids play in a league where lead offs are allowed, there's a bunch you can teach them that, at the very least, will provide some interesting diversions during practice and at the very most, get your young pitchers out of some very tough jams.

The first of these is directed toward getting the runner at 2nd base. The middle infielders, whose job it is to hold the runner on, should be taught to alternate going to the bag and back to their position, whether there's a play on or not.

(continued)

On this Pick-Off play, the shortstop comes to the bag , touches and returns to his position, but does so **in front of** the runner. The pitcher is looking at the catcher. The working assumption here is that the runner will extend his lead as he sees the shortstop come off the bag in front of him. The catcher looks for **"Daylight" between the two.** When he sees it, he **drops his glove,** as a sign for the 2nd baseman to break to the bag, and for the pitcher to turn and throw.

A variation on this play can be used when the other team is trying to bunt the runner to 3rd. When the shortstop comes off the bag in front of the runner, he's **breaks toward 3rd base,** as if the "Wheel Play" was in effect. The runner, eager to get a good jump, should follow. The catcher drops the glove, the 2nd baseman breaks, the pitchers turns and throws. The umpire calls him "Out". Nothin' to it.

A third play is used in **1st-and-3rd** situations. The pitcher turns as if to pick-off the runner at 3rd base. He fakes the throw, pauses, then looks to see if the runner has extended his lead off 1st base. This is called the "Turtle" play, because the pitcher arches his back in the shape of a turtle's shell to help sell the play. The 3rd baseman can also help "sell" this play by going through the motions of catching the throw from the pitcher. The pitcher **breaks contact** with the mound with the trailing leg while faking to 3rd. This is something he'd do normally on a Pick-Off attempt, but if he gets excited and forgets, then tries to go to 1st base with the throw, the umpire's going to call a balk. The good news is that, since he has broken contact he **doesn't** have to make the throw to 1st base. Other Pick-Off plays can be triggered by counts, verbal commands or signals from the bench.

Here are three plays you can use to defense a 1st and 3rd steal situation:

(1) The catcher fakes to 2nd, looks to 3rd, and throws if warranted.

(2) The shortstop or 2nd baseman comes in halfway between the mound and 2nd to cut-off the throw and gets the runner going home.

(3) The catcher throws through to 2nd, usually with two outs.

Teach your kids that throwing a pitch is **not an option** when a Pick-Off play is on. Either the pitcher throws to the bag or backs off the rubber. Infielders make a pitcher look good. It's a Cardinal Sin to make them look bad by throwing home when infielders are out of position.

PITCHER VS. HITTER
Baseball Predator/Prey Relationship

Some words about the special Predator/Prey relationship at the heart of the game itself, that which exists between Pitcher and Hitter:

WHAT THE PITCHER LOOKS FOR, IF THE HITTER...

... Stands **too far back** in the batter's box, he's looking for the fastball. Get him with the off-speed stuff.

... Stands **too far up** in the box, he's thinking off-speed pitch all the way. Bust him with the fastball.

... Has **both elbows down** at his side, he's a ground ball hitter and will not have the leverage needed to get on top of the ball that's up in the strike zone. Pitch him above the waist.

... Has his **arms extended** too much over home plate, he will not be able to hit the ball to the opposite field with any power. On the other hand, the only ball he usually can pull is down-and-in. Pitch him away and make sure to position your fielders accordingly.

... Is **right-handed,** he likes the ball above the waist. One of baseball's Universal Truths. Is **left-handed,** he likes the ball down. Another Universal Truth.

... Has a **Closed stance** (front foot closer to home plate), he has a diagonal Hitting Zone. His first pitch of choice is a ball up-and-away. The second, a ball down-and-in. Work him the opposite. Especially with fastballs up-and-in.

... Has an **Open stance** (front foot away), he's looking for a fastball he can punch to the opposite field or an inside curve ball he can pull. Stay with fastballs on the inner half of the plate or curve balls away.

... Has an **especially long stride,** he likes the ball down in the strike zone. Remember, the longer the stride the more the hands and head drop. He won't have enough leverage to drive a high pitch very far.

(continued)

... Carries his hands **above the shoulders,** keep the ball down. Carries his hands **at the waist,** keep the ball up. Power comes from moving the hands forward, not up and down, so no matter which extreme position the batter uses, if he hits the ball it won't go very far.

...Does not **catch up to the 1st fastball** you threw him, keeping throwing them until he proves that he can. Don't make the mistake of "speeding up the bat" by throwing something off-speed. **"Make Them Hit the Fastball"** are five words that should be etched in the mind of every young pitcher.

... Swings at a pitch **out of the strike zone** early in the count, expand the strike zone on him by throwing the next pitch even farther away. Make him prove he knows the strike zone before you throw one over the plate.

... Hit a **home run** against you the last time he was up, embarrassing you in front of your parents, your grandparents, your little sister, and that cute girl in the stands, the one you've had a crush on since kindergarten, don't be afraid to face him the next time he comes to bat. Chances are, the home run was more a product of **your mistake** than his talent. Learn from the experience. Throw something different. Remember, the **advantage is** always with the pitcher.

WHAT THE HITTER LOOKS FOR, IF THE PITCHER...

... Likes to change his grip a lot, pay close attention to which pitch follows which grip. If the pitcher's careless enough to telegraph his pitches, make him pay for the mistake.

...Throws the ball **especially hard,** look for the 1st pitch that's down in the strike zone and go after it. High fastballs have a nasty tendency to rise even higher. Choke up a bit, or use a lighter bat. Whatever you do, **don't move back in the box.** Every pitch has movement and the farther back you are in the box, the more the ball's going to move before it gets to you, whether it's a fastball or a curve.

...Throws the ball **especially slow,** be patient and wait for your pitch. Pitchers like this survive on location and changing patterns. But sooner or later he'll make a mistake. That's the pitch you want to hit.

... Pitches from **3rd base side** of the mound, look for balls on that side of the plate. Same for pitchers who work from the **1st base side.**

... Has **good control** and is always around the strike zone, be more aggressive. There's no lonelier moment in baseball than standing at the plate, game on the line, with a no-ball, two-strike count.

... Likes to throw everything on the **outer half of the plate,** relax, don't try to pull the ball. Just use an Inside-Out swing and punch the ball to the opposite field. In many ways, the easiest pitch to hit is one that's up-and-away, just so long as you don't try to do too much with it.

... Likes to **pitch inside,** be ready for the fastball - this guy's coming to get you. Let your hands work "inside the ball". And remember his name, chances are he'll be pitching for some time to come.

... Likes to **throw the curve ball,** just try to hit it back up the middle. And smile, because this guy's doing you a favor. The biggest mistake young pitchers make is falling in love with off-speed pitches. But that's his problem, not yours.

... Is one of those **big, slow-moving guys,** make him field his position. Drop a bunt now and then. Even if you're unsuccessful, you've given him one more thing to think about and every ounce of concentration you can drain from a pitcher is a pound of opportunity for you.

... Takes **too much time** between pitches, step out of the box until he's ready to pitch to you. Don't let him ruin your concentration, or your timing, by making you wait on him.

... Pitches **too quickly,** step out of the box until you're ready for him. Make him wait on you.

... **Struck you out** the last time you came up, embarrassing you in front of your parents, your grandparents, your little sister, and the cute girl in the stands, **relax.** And remember what pitch he got you out on. Chances are he'll come right back to it this time. Even though the advantage is with the pitcher, the most dramatics moments in the game usually are reserved for the hitter. **This time, you get to be the hero.**

Chapter 9

Coaching/Trouble Shooting

Maddening it is for a coach, and disheartening for a player, when everything right starts to go wrong. Worse still, is the natural inclination for bad habits to multiply on each other - especially when dealing with kids. Drop one fly ball and three more are sure to follow. Walk one batter and before you know it, the bases are loaded.

At times like these, least of all things that you want to do as a coach is give up hope. Mistakes made on the baseball field usually are born not of luck, fate or fortune, but of bad habits. Yes, bad habits are hard to break. Our grandmothers told us that. Hard, but not impossible.

Not when you use tricks like these...

WHEN YOUR PITCHERS CAN'T THROW STRIKES
Send Them to the Strings

When kids can't throw strikes, they almost always make things more difficult for themselves by pinching the strike zone even more. Aiming the ball. Not following through. Trying too hard to make a perfect pitch.

This is the time to remind young pitchers that the **strike zone really is a pretty big place,** not defined by the shape of home plate or the size of the catcher's glove. It's an area, as wide as home plate (17 inches) and as tall as the distance between a batter's armpits and his knees. When understood this way, even the most discouraged kids can be taught just how much room they have to make something good happen. A visual aid helps make this point crystal clear. Something called "The Strings".

(continued)

The Strings have been around spring training camps for more than a half-century and are a great tool for pitchers, no matter the age or experience. Take two tall, thin pieces of wood - tomato stakes will do, just so long as there are at least four feet long - and anchor them on **either side of home plate.** They should be at least four feet apart. Now take two long pieces of string and connect them to the stakes, one running horizontally along the top of the strike zone, the other at the bottom. Take two smaller pieces and tie them vertically to the long pieces, directly over the edges of home plate.

Behold, the strike zone.

Teach your kids to just throw the ball **through** the Strings and not to try and aim at one spot. What should follow are strikes, bunches and bunches of them. Thrown easily and effortlessly by a young pitcher who's relaxed by the knowledge there's a lot of room to work with.

The Strings also can be used to teach kids to throw to the **Corridors** of home plate, by attaching other strings to section off the strike zone either vertically or horizontally - inside/outside, high/low. You can make the Strings even more visible for your kids by spraying them with some kind of day-glo paint.

WHEN YOUR HITTERS CAN'T HIT THE BALL
Send Them to the Mirror

Don't be angry, impatient or confused when Johnny can't hit. He's not alone. Even the best hitters fail 70% of the time. As it is with pitchers who can't throw strikes, the problem usually is something simple and easy to correct. But it's also likely to be something best understood **when seen for himself.** For that, send him to the nearest mirror.

Setting your kids up in front of the mirror is a great way to help them see and understand for themselves what the problem is and how easy it is to correct. It also helps build **"muscle memory"-** the natural reflex instinct so important to athletes - when the body takes over even before the mind has a chance to tell it to.

HERE ARE SOME THINGS THAT SHOULD BE EASY TO SEE:

That the **shoulders** stay level all the way through the swing. The **back elbow** is at roughly a 45-degree angle to the ground. The stride is short - no more than 6 to 10 inches. The **front elbow** stays in tight to the body during the swing. On landing, the **weight** is over the ball of the front foot, creating a stiff front leg to hit against.

The palm of the top hand is up at the point of impact. The **wrists roll over** only afterward. The **hips rotate,** serving as the "trigger" for all that power generated by the lower body. The **heel of the back foot** is up at the end of the swing. The **front side stays Closed** all the way through the Hitting Zone.

Once your kids have learned to feel comfortable with their swing after some "slow-motion" time in front of the mirror, have them take some swings with **their eyes closed,** telling them to "feel" each part of the swing unfold and let that "muscle memory" take over. Just don't let them do all this with a bat in their hands. The last thing you want to hear is the sound of breaking glass.

WHEN YOUR KIDS CAN'T CATCH GROUNDERS
Have Them Take Off the Gloves

An easy way to help bring back the correct mechanics for fielding ground balls is by having your kids take of their glove. Some kids tend to use a baseball glove as a shield, others as a giant net. Neither is a way to promote either good mechanics or high fielding percentages.

Have your kids stand a few feet away, in the Ready Position and **softly bounce** some ground balls their way. You can use either baseballs or tennis balls. Make sure they keep their **hands lower than the ball.** That they **point the bill of the cap** at the ball, following the ball all the way into the hands. And that each ball is fielded between the shoulders and with the elbows out front, acting as the shock absorbers.

Catching the ball bare-handed is a good way to help kids remember the **"Thumbs & Pinkies"** Rule of fielding the ball. It also promotes that natural cushioning action, bringing the hands back a few inches on impact and creating those "soft hands" baseball scouts love to see.

(continued)

WHEN YOUR KIDS CAN'T CATCH FLYBALLS
Time to Pick Up a Racquet

Anyone who's ever been on the receiving end of a flyball knows that - like snowflakes - no two are ever alike. They come at **different angles,** with **different speed, varying degrees of spin,** and all with the intent of causing great bodily harm to a young player who thinks that what's happening at this instant constitutes the worst moment of his entire life.

Catching fly balls - like catching ground balls - is the product of **good mechanics.** Not catching them is the product of **fear.** To help take that fear away from your kids, put down the bat, and go find a tennis racquet.

Using a tennis ball and racquet to hit to your kids gives you **two quick advantages: (1)** Helps kids concentrate on the mechanics, and, **(2)** Allows them to do so without the fear of being hurt. After a few tries, especially if you've ever played the game of tennis before, you'll find how easy it is to **impart spin to the ball,** making it hook or slice, giving it topspin or backspin, all in an attempt to simulate what fly balls can do en route to an outfielder.

Using the tennis racquet also is a great way to teach all of your kids the basic defensive rule that a **fly ball hit toward the line will drift toward the line.** A ball pulled down the left field line by a right-handed hitter will hook toward that line. A ball sliced down the right field line by that same hitter will fade toward that line. Opposite rules apply for fly balls hit by left-handed hitters.

This also helps you to remember that it's best to position your opposite-field players **shallower** than those on the "pull" side of the field. When a hitter pulls the ball, he's hit it with his entire body. When he slices it, it's with his arms and as a result, the ball's not going to go as far.

Part of the challenge and the reward of working with kids is how it allows you to be resourceful in creating **simple solutions** to things that can seem so overwhelming to kids.

Each of the tips mentioned here was nothing more than the product of sudden inspiration brought on by temporary despair. Home remedies, if you will, put to the test on the field of play. What happens when urgent need is met with gentle understanding. Chances are, you'll be able to come up with a whole chapter's worth of these yourself, whenever need and opportunity meet at the same place, at the same time.

In the end, understand that one of the things that separates good coaches from the rest is **anticipation,** whether it's trouble-shooting away problems during practice or planning three batters ahead during the game. Understand, too, that part of the job means accepting the fact that not everything you do is going to work out the way you planned. Just give it your best shot. Have fun with it.

That's what you're there for.

AND REMEMBER, IT'S ONLY A GAME...

The Last Word...

The town of Sherman Oaks, California, in which I had the pure pleasure of growing up in the '50s, was just large enough to support a very grand total of four Little League fields, situated together as corners of a perfect square, near the intersection of Magnolia Avenue and Hazeltine Street, forming the heart of this suburban community that, with its soda shops and Mom & Pop grocery stores, seemed at times to have been brought forth from the fertile soil of Norman Rockwell's imagination.

The baseball fields served as spring and summertime common ground for those of us whose parents shared the good sense and greater fortune to choose this place to begin the cycle of work, home, and family that so defined American life in the postwar years.

Today, it isn't just the sights, smells and sounds of Saturdays spent working a path from ball game to ball game that are remembered, there is also the certain knowledge of lessons that have lasted a lifetime.

That both victory and defeat are to be shared. That each lasts only a moment. That life, as exampled by a child's game crafted from leather and wood, mixed with generous amounts of green grass, blue sky and sunshine, is about redemption. Teamwork. And playing by the rules.

I have concluded, after years of experience and more sleepless nights than I wish to count, that teaching baseball to kids demands a person of emotional makeup equal parts George Patton and Mr. Rogers. Without the former, the learning process is lost in a fog of confusion. Without the latter, it ceases to be fun, and therefore of little value at all.

Baseball is not a simple game, though it often is portrayed as such. It has as many twists and turns, opportunities won and opportunities lost, as can be found in any other theatre of life. All of which conspire to demand the very best, in character and skill, of those who play it. A similar test lies in store for those who teach it.

From all of this comes the realization that when working with kids, it's not **what** you say, it's **how** you say it that counts. A distinction that can be as easily described as the difference between "Way to go, Johnny", and "Way to keep your shoulders squared, Johnny". With the first message comes support. With the second, support plus education. Which equals wisdom. On the part of both adult and child.

At the close of each season I manage to pretty well convince myself that - finally, at last, once and for all - I've learned just about everything there is to know about the game. A presumption usually born more of fatigue than self-assurance. One that lies in hibernation only until the following spring, when the cycle renews itself again. And every day brings with it new experience, new understanding, and new reward.

So, don't feel bad when your own pool of wisdom runs as dry as the Gobi desert. Take a moment. Refresh yourself in the cool waters of memories that promise never to quite fade away. Think about why you came. What brings you back, again and again.

It's baseball. And being a parent. Both on display in their purest form, every time you pick up a ball and glove... and play the game.

Baseball.

Have a great season,

Don Marsh
San Diego
June, 2004

Special Moments
Diary for Parents & Kids

DATE	SPECIAL MOMENTS

Special Moments
Diary for Parents & Kids

DATE	SPECIAL MOMENTS

Special Moments
Diary for Parents & Kids

DATE	SPECIAL MOMENTS

Special Moments
Diary for Parents & Kids

DATE	SPECIAL MOMENTS

Special Moments
Diary for Parents & Kids

DATE	SPECIAL MOMENTS

Special Moments
Diary for Parents & Kids

DATE	SPECIAL MOMENTS

Special Moments
Diary for Parents & Kids

DATE	SPECIAL MOMENTS

Special Moments
Diary for Parents & Kids

DATE	SPECIAL MOMENTS

Special Moments
Diary for Parents & Kids

DATE	SPECIAL MOMENTS

Special Moments
Diary for Parents & Kids

DATE	SPECIAL MOMENTS

Special Moments
Diary for Parents & Kids

DATE	SPECIAL MOMENTS

Special Moments
Diary for Parents & Kids

DATE	SPECIAL MOMENTS

Special Moments
Diary for Parents & Kids

DATE	SPECIAL MOMENTS

Special Moments
Diary for Parents & Kids

DATE	SPECIAL MOMENTS

RE-ORDER FORM

Price: $11.95 per book, plus $2.35 Shipping & Handling.

☐ **YES!!! Please send my copy today.**

I've enclosed a check or money order (US dollars only) in the amount of $14.30. (CA residents add $.93 sales tax)

Send to: (print or type)

NAME _____

ADDRESS_____

CITY_____ STATE_____ ZIP_____

TELEPHONE (OPTIONAL/IN CASE OF QUESTIONS) (_____) _____

Send To:
101 Things You Can Teach Your Kids About Baseball
c/o Campbell Marsh Communications
5010 Caminito Exquisito, San Diego, CA 92130-2850
Phone: (858) 792-6553   Fax: (858) 792-6553

SPECIAL TEAM DISCOUNT

SAVE $2 by Ordering Two Books or More!!! ($9.95 per book)

SAVE $3 by Ordering Six Books or More!!! ($ 8.95 per book)

Enclosed is my check or money order in the amount of $_____

(Team Price: $9.95, 2 - 5 books; $8.95 six books or more, plus $2.35 Shipping & Handling)

Please Copy This Section for Volume Orders

TEAM NAME _____

ADDITIONAL NAME(S) _____

ADDRESS(ES) _____

CITY_____ STATE _____ ZIP _____

Third Edition

101 Things
You Can Teach
Your Kids
About Baseball

With Advanced Pitching Section

Pitching, Infielding/Outfielding, Catching, Hitting, Bunting/Baserunning, Diary Pages, 4 Chapters for Coaches, And More!!

By Don Marsh

Book design and illustrations by: Ann Campbell

3rd Edition Copyright 2004, Campbell Marsh Communications.

ISBN 0-9647420-7-1
Third Edition